Evaluating Bilingual Education Programs

Bernard H. Cohen

TEACHING RESOURCES CORPORATION
50 Pond Park Road
Hingham, MA 02043

About the Author

Bernard Cohen and the staff of Bernard Cohen Research and Development, Inc., have assessed the impact of bilingual education in more than 50 different bilingual education programs from Caribou, Maine, to Los Angeles, California. Using 12 years of research and evaluation in bilingual education, Mr. Cohen has identified practical evaluation procedures and workable instructional models.

In addition to serving as President of BCR&D, Mr. Cohen has taught bilingual language arts in teacher-training programs and served as special consultant to National Geographic, Children's Television Workshop, state departments of education, and other organizations attempting to meet the needs of children with limited English-speaking abilities.

Preface

Since the late sixties, school systems have been implementing and evaluating bilingual-education programs with an ever-increasing emphasis on accountability. At the same time, colleges and universities have acquired more sophisticated knowledge about learning, especially in the instructional areas of language, reading, and linguistics. Developers of commercially available instruments and practitioners in the field have been hard pressed to keep pace with progress in the linguistic sciences. This book presents a nontechnical, practical approach to bilingual-program evaluation for these practitioners.

Applicability and usefulness have guided the selection of material for the text. For example, rather than discussing dozens of acceptable research models and quasi-research designs, the book presents simple models that can be readily implemented in most public school systems, classrooms, and research departments. This practical, goal-related set of procedures is designed to assist local administrators and teachers in conducting an ongoing evaluation of their bilingual programs in several key areas. Moreover, these procedures should become part of all sophisticated evaluation models, so that those models are more relevant to operational bilingual education.

Contents

Appendices

Introduction

In 1968 HEW's Office of Education inaugurated the "era of accountability" by attaching program-evaluation requirements to ESEA, Title VII bilingual-education programs. Immediately, school personnel began looking to publishers, universities, and their own research units for assistance in the development and implementation of evaluation activities. Unfortunately, no bilingual-education evaluation models were to be found.

Although bilingual instruction has been the focus of much attention in recent years, it is by no means a new development in the United States. Before World War I, many language groups instituted various forms of bilingual education in both public and private schools: French in New England and Louisiana; Spanish in New Mexico; and German in the Midwest. Furthermore, some language groups established monolingual schools in which the native language was the primary instructional medium, with English taught only as a subject. With the coming of World War I and a sharp increase in nationalistic fervor, instruction in languages other than English was considered by many to be unpatriotic. At times, such instruction was even banned. Nevertheless, by mid-century schools in various parts of the country began turning to bilingual education as an effective way to meet the educational needs of the children they served. Dade County in Florida and New York City began implementing programs in the early sixties. At the same time, several districts in the Southwest began strengthening and expanding already-existing dual-language programs, programs that had been dormant or underutilized for years. The success of these efforts rejuvenated bilingual education in the United States, and programs have multiplied rapidly in the sixties and seventies.

Since its rebirth, bilingual education has posed some unique instructional problems. New requirements, terminologies, and concepts must be mastered. Teachers and project administrators are now asked to develop process objectives along with product goals. Educators must design programs that provide both dominant-language and second-language instruction, and educational researchers must develop data-collection and analysis techniques to measure a series of previously untried and still somewhat undefined pedagogical processes. Evaluation techniques to assess these emerging concepts are often more elusive than the educational activities themselves. Frequently, evaluators find themselves working with confusing data in an inconsistent evaluation framework.

The evaluation requirements for ESEA, Title VII, and locally funded bilingual-education projects are grounded in some of the most sensible and sensitive reasons for accountability ever produced. All too often, experimental programs are measured against a comparison program or model. Their worth is purely relative; if they fall short, they are not likely to get a second chance. In the case of bilingual education, the purposes for evaluation have been somewhat different. Evaluators are asked to identify program strengths and weaknesses, to make recommendations, and to contribute to the refinement of an emerging educational model. This *should* be the purpose of all program evaluations. Regrettably, however, school evaluation activities have yet to be viewed as a totally constructive process.

The evaluation philosophies expressed in Title VII have served as a model for this text. The approaches discussed enable a bilingual-education program to conduct an ongoing needs assessment by continuously identifying strengths and weaknesses. Furthermore, the techniques outlined foster a positive rather than a negative attitude toward evaluation. For example, in this model, the purpose of teacher evaluation is not to identify individual strengths and weaknesses as a basis for hiring and firing decisions. Rather, teacher evaluation is an integral component of a comprehensive approach to program evaluation, an approach that builds on strengths and remedies weaknesses.

In order to evaluate a bilingual-education program within

this affirmative framework, an evaluator must be willing to involve teachers, administrators, and parents in the development of program objectives and in the planning of evaluation activities. The evaluator must also be willing to utilize parents and other community representatives to assist with data collection. Finally, the evaluator must abandon a purist approach to educational research in favor of procedures that may be less than totally scientific in derivation. Such procedures, because they are based on the operational processes of bilingual education, are often more accurate than traditional procedures. This is not to say that evaluators of bilingual programs should relinquish scientism. Rather, they should be willing to use those instruments or procedures, regardless of origin, that provide the most useful and valid information to teachers and administrators.

A comprehensive approach to bilingual evaluation requires management skills that are not usually associated with program evaluation. Educational projects frequently utilize planning, communications, and coordination procedures, systems that should also be used by program-evaluation teams. A bilingual-program evaluation, if it is not organized, cannot possibly be diagnostic and linked to decision making. It is important to remember that the diagnostic aspects of an evaluation usually tend to be most helpful in the year-to-year upgrading of services to students.

The author has worked primarily with Spanish-English programs; however, much of the information presented is transferable to other language and cultural groups sharing similar purposes and problems. Regardless of the language or cultural group being served, instructional products and processes may be measured in like fashion.

As a final introductory note, the reader should remember that this book is a nontechnical guide. Statistical technicalities and some of the more sophisticated methodologies are beyond its scope. In order to evaluate program effectiveness adequately and to ensure that evaluation designs meet local and federal requirements for evaluation, projects should work in concert with educational evaluators and classroom practitioners, keeping evaluation practical rather than elusively esoteric.

1 Purposes of Bilingual-Program Evaluation Designs

An evaluation plan for a bilingual-education program should not be a series of research activities conducted merely for the sake of research. To develop an evaluation that is directly related to program services, project administrators should ensure that each evaluation process has a specific, student-related purpose. In this way, the evaluation of a bilingual program is more apt to be research for action rather than research in isolation.

Data should be collected in the following areas:

☐ Dominant-language reading readiness and learning readiness (prekindergarten and kindergarten)

☐ General ability (first grade)

☐ Dominant-language reading (in the language of reading instruction)

☐ Second-language reading (only students receiving second-language reading instruction)

☐ Oral language development in both instructional languages (Spanish language arts and ESL)

☐ Mathematics (in the language of instruction)

- [ ] Self-concept
- [ ] Teacher effectiveness
- [ ] Teacher aide effectiveness
- [ ] Curriculum materials
- [ ] Program management
- [ ] Staff training
- [ ] Community involvement
- [ ] Subjects such as science, social studies, etc. (junior and senior high school)

Additional topics can be added according to individual program needs. However, with the budget and time limitations confronting most evaluators, priorities must be established. If, for example, program evaluation has shown that a particular group of elementary-school youngsters is consistently demonstrating anticipated increases in mathematics over a period of years, the evaluator of that program might temporarily discontinue data collection and analysis in math and become more diagnostic in reading, self-concept, parent awareness, or other less successful program areas. On the other hand, when data-collection activities are discontinued, the possibility of a longitudinal study in that particular area is limited. To prevent this from happening, program administrators should realize that eliminating a specific area of measurement from an evaluation plan does not necessarily eliminate the related testing and storage of data.

Using the data gathered in the areas cited at the beginning of this chapter, a bilingual-program evaluation should:

- [ ] Introduce teachers, aides, and parents to program goals and student needs
- [ ] Foster two-way accountability between teachers and administrators
- [ ] Identify instructional strengths and weaknesses by subject, grade, language, and instructional level (average, below average, etc.)
- [ ] Serve as a management tool for decision making related to program processes (instructional format, curriculum materials, inservice, etc.)
- [ ] Meet the informational needs of all concerned stakeholders (administrators, teachers, aides, parents, and students)

These objectives can be met only if teachers, administrators, and parents are involved in the evaluation process. Teachers must be given an opportunity to set criterion references for end-of-year performance levels, and parents must have a chance to express their own informational needs to the evaluator. Administrators should discuss previously identified program weaknesses and future program plans with the evaluator so that the evaluation design can serve all student groups and program areas in a diagnostic fashion. Finally, if all five purposes are to be achieved, especially those aimed at identifying process strengths and weaknesses, there must be a free flow of communication between the evaluation team and the program throughout the academic year. An interim or a final evaluation report is insufficient; observations must be communicated on a weekly or monthly basis.

2 Suggested Research Designs

Evaluation models, if they are to be feasible, must be based on edu-political realities rather than abstract research designs. In the day-to-day world of education, many processes related to program and school management do not easily conform to the parameters of a research design. In addition, the sociopolitical characteristics of a community and a school can further complicate the development of a research model by restricting the use of comparison groups, ethnic or linguistic analyses, and certain process-evaluation activities. Practical administrators and evaluators should review alternative research plans with teachers, subject-area representatives, administrators, and other stakeholders before finalizing a model. In this way, local needs and scientific needs may be weighed and given priorities.

A few definitions are necessary before going on. The term *control group* cannot be loosely used. During recent years, researchers and evaluators have substituted the term *comparison group*, because scientifically controlled variables are nearly impossible to arrange in most programs. The use of comparison groups gives evaluators little more than an educated estimate, since such variables as intelligence, attendance, and years in the United States cannot usually be controlled. Still, it is more accurate and diagnostic to use comparison groups than to use nothing at all.

Pre-Post, Program-Comparison Design

The most accurate design for assessing a bilingual program calls for pretesting and posttesting program and comparison students at each grade level within each participating school. For a number of reasons, this design is rarely used.

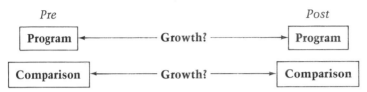

Fig. 2.1 *Pre-post, program-comparison design (similar groups)*

In order to implement this model, a program evaluator should meet as many of the following criteria as possible:

☐ Participating students are randomly selected.

☐ Pretest score averages of comparison groups and program groups are not significantly different.

☐ Comparison groups at each grade level within each school building are used.

☐ If a program is serving an entire school building, a comparison group at another school, with similar socioeconomic situations, is used.

☐ Comparison classes receive instruction totally in English and do not participate in other bilingual programs.

Quite often, circumstances make comparison groups less than perfect. For example, if several parents deny permission for their children to participate in a program, the research may be strongly biased, making comparison groups inappropriate. A comparison bias also exists if students are placed in a program solely on the basis of language or educational need. Although it is not wrong to group students on this basis, it is wrong to make intergroup comparisons if the educational strengths and weaknesses of the two groups are dissimilar.

Finally, teachers of comparison-group classes sometimes resent being relegated to "other group" status and feel that the research is aimed at proving them incompetent. In such a situation, the negative effect on staff morale outweighs the potential gains one might derive from a pre-post, intergroup design. Quite often, researchers have an opportunity to select comparison classes by using city-wide testing records. In this way, comparison teachers are never publicly identified and are never aware of their involvement. There is no need to name either students or teachers in an evaluation report; they should serve only to provide comparative data for measuring the effectiveness of a bilingual program or classroom. Use of city-wide testing records is usually limited to English reading and math. To arrange an intergroup design for Spanish reading (or for any language other than English), an evaluator must establish a relationship with principals and supervisors of nonparticipating schools that also serve Hispanic children.

The instructional goals incorporated into a program-comparison design are often destined for failure because they call for bilingual classes to outperform comparison groups. This is an unrealistic expectation. Researchers and project administrators should instead consider striving for the null hypothesis, especially during a program's first few years. Bilingual classes can be expected to move ahead of nonprogram classes only after a few years of program development and refinement. If bilingual-program children do as well as nonprogram groups or show no significant difference after only one year, the bilingual program should be commended.

Quite often, bilingual-education programs serve all the limited-English-speaking students at a particular grade level within a school. Even in this situation, one need not completely rule out the use of comparison groups. If the nonprogram children are not limited in English-speaking ability and are, therefore, "advantaged" insofar as language arts is concerned, intergroup comparison objectives can be established. These objectives should call for a reduction in the gap between the two groups' pretest scores, particularly in areas such as English reading and oral language arts. In other subjects — mathematics, for example — the bilingual classes may strive to be at or above the level of comparison classes after two or three years of program involvement, with smaller gaps between the two groups each consecutive year.

Posttest-Only Design

Although comparison groups work best in the pre-post design, intergroup comparisons using only posttests are perfectly valid if program participants are randomly selected. Total randomization ensures that the groups will be at least somewhat similar even though their pretest scores have not been determined.

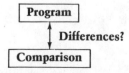

Fig. 2.2 *Posttest-only design*

In addition to random participation, this design requires at least 20–25 students in each group at each grade level. The larger the groups of program and nonprogram students, the greater the likelihood of pretest similarity. Of course, the model also has obvious disadvantages, such as lack of diagnostic data.

In a two-group posttest-only design, the comparison group cannot be totally composed of monolingual English students. If such a group were used, student selection for the groups would not be totally random.

Post-Post Design

Program evaluators have also been able to compare Spanish-dominant children with English-dominant children if end-of-year testing is conducted on an annual basis. The goal in this case is a reduction in the gap between program Spanish-dominant and nonprogram English-dominant students. Each group's previous-year data is compared with current-year data. Of course, the evaluator is actually using the previous year's posttesting and the current year's posttesting to establish a pre-post model. If a significant percentage of program students remain in the bilingual classes for a period of two or three years, a longitudinal study of the program's impact is possible. In this way, a rather weak evaluation model can become a quite useful assessment tool.

Gap-Reduction Model with Dissimilar Groups

Evaluation reports based on intergroup comparisons must be sensitively written, especially if one is comparing a limited-English-speaking group to monolingual English speakers. This type of comparison should be used only when linguistically similar groups are unavailable. Furthermore, comparisons should be limited to the following areas:

- ☐ Math (testing in each group's dominant language and for computation skills only)
- ☐ Reading readiness (testing in each child's dominant language)
- ☐ General ability (testing in each child's dominant language or in both languages)
- ☐ Native-language reading (only skills that are appropriate to the child's developmental level; testing in each child's dominant language)

☐ English reading (only to show a reduction in the gap between the two groups)

Growth in these learning areas can be measured when the two groups are of similar age and grade levels. If the nonprogram group is ahead of the program group at the beginning of the year, comparisons can be made if the goals call for a reduction in the gap between the groups or gains that see no furthering of the differences.

Fig. 2.3 *Gap-reduction model*

Evaluation Techniques

Several techniques can be used to obtain data. First, by studying scores on standardized tests in English reading and mathematics, the evaluator can compare growth in grade-equivalency months to the number of months between pre- and posttesting. This approach has one disadvantage: it is not always possible to pretest students early enough. In certain kinds of learning activities, a considerable amount of learning takes place at the very beginning of the school year. If the students are not pretested until mid-October or later, a bilingual program may be underrated. The measured growth between pre- and posttesting may not equal the chronological growth or the actual growth for the year. Standardized tests have one major advantage: bilingual programs may use a post-post design, requiring testing only at the end of each year along with end-of-year analyses that compare the gap between the program children and the norm references, looking for reductions in the gap between program and norm scores over each year's time.

If a program does not use comparison groups and standardized tests, evaluators usually rely on inferential statistics. Programs also use inferential statistics if the norms for a standardized test (grade equivalencies, percentiles, etc.) were established on population groups in some way dissimilar to the population being tested. Whatever the reason for use, inferential statistics determine the degree to which a group's growth is statistically significant. The term *statistical significance* describes an indication of probability, or the degree to which average growth between pre- and posttesting was due to learning rather than mere chance.

Inferential calculations such as the t-test involve a series of computations that take into account each child's growth, the group's average growth, the standard deviation, and other mathematical factors. The result of a t-test computation is the probability associated with a certain value of the t-statistic for that number of subjects. If the end product of a t-test is .05, the evaluator subtracts that figure from 100 and says that he or she is 95 percent certain that growth was due to an educational program or treatment rather than to maturation or chance.

Unfortunately, although the use of inferential statistics is supported by HEW and most state departments of education, there are many weaknesses inherent in this method. For example, consider a group whose pretest mean (average) score was 25 and whose posttest mean score increased to 45. Given a large enough population, this increase would probably be statistically significant. However, if there were 200 items on the test, we might not be satisfied with this growth rate. There is a difference between statistical significance and importance — in other words, a statistical result is not always a meaningful result. In order to avoid misuse of all statistical methods, the evaluator must, in every case, determine if the method is appropriate for the collected data.

Inferential statistics and the various analytical approaches (t-test, chi square, f-scores, etc.) have another drawback. Educators and community representatives who do not have a background in statistics or tests and measurement may have difficulty interpreting statistical results. Therefore, the evaluator must translate these results into a form that can be readily understood by the intended audience.

Statistical analysis appropriate to criterion-referenced approaches to testing and evaluation is growing in popularity. Ordinarily the term *criterion* in criterion-referenced testing refers to a certain skill, mastery of which is demonstrated by completing specified tasks. Lately, the term has also been used in reference to end-of-year scores predicted at the beginning of the year. For example, a program may call for a growth rate of six months or may use an approach to data analysis called *anticipated gain rate*. This approach is quite individualized, but is generally considered useful only above the fourth grade. Anticipated gain rate is calculated by dividing each pre-test score by the number of years in school. For example, the average gain rate of a child in the sixth grade with a 3.0 reading score is 0.5 per year. One criterion approach requires that each child show a gain rate that exceeds his or her previous average gain rate; others call for specific increases in the average gain rate. The percentage of increase in the average gain rate is usually arbitrary and subject to change annually based on the previous year's history. This makes the approach somewhat less than totally objective. Program evaluators can reduce the subjectivity of this technique if they involve teachers, reading specialists, and other local stakeholders in decisions regarding the required percentage of gain-rate increase.

When an average gain rate or an accelerated gain rate is used, each student's average gain must be computed prior to the full implementation of the research design. Thus, the evaluator must work with individual scores rather than group averages. This tends to foster a more individualized program and provides teachers with individualized gain-rate data. The chart presented in Appendix A can be used to tally data in this fashion. The evaluator records each child's pretest score, his or her average gain rate per year, and the individual gain-rate objective for that particular child. The individual objective should equal the average gain rate or exceed it by a certain percentage. The final column on the chart should be marked after the post-test scores have been computed to determine if the objective was achieved.

3 Developing Performance Objectives for Bilingual Programs

Although most administrators and evaluators have taken courses and attended workshops on the development of performance objectives,* a text on evaluating bilingual programs would be incomplete if it did not briefly review approaches for developing specific and measurable goals. Without a series of well-defined performance objectives, evaluation models and data-collection procedures are likely to be haphazard or unfocused at best. Furthermore, it is difficult, if not impossible, to discuss program effectiveness objectively without predetermined, specifically stated goals.

Much has been written about performance objectives, structural hierarchies, and taxonomic procedures. A school system can borrow from several approaches to develop an evaluation design that is suitable for its evaluation needs. A program's success or performance criteria should be established prior to the implementation of program and evaluation activities. These performance objectives should:

---

*The terms *performance objectives, goals, behavioral objectives,* and *benchmarks* are used interchangeably to represent specific statements of anticipated outcomes.

- [ ] Provide a skeleton for the development of program proposals, component designs, and instructional activities
- [ ] Specifically identify teaching philosophies and instructional areas for participating teachers
- [ ] Inform parents, teachers, and students about the expectations of the program developers

The chart provided in Appendix B is a useful tool for ensuring that a program's performance objectives meet all these purposes. A sample completed chart appears on page 16. At first, there may seem to be too many pigeonholes, too many blanks to fill. However, as program personnel establish objectives, communicate those objectives to parents and teachers, and develop instructional models and program proposals, they will find that the chart provides structure, organization, and clarity. Equally important, it establishes a direct relationship between the instructional program and program evaluation.

Before going any further, a few brief definitions related to the sample chart are in order:

- [ ] Target population: the student group that is expected to meet the stated objective
- [ ] Desired behavior: a general description of the instructional area addressed by the objective
- [ ] Performance level: a specific description of the level at which the desired behavior must be shown; a preidentification of program-success criteria
- [ ] Operational condition: any occurrences that must take place in order for the desired behavior and performance levels to be accomplished
- [ ] Instrument: a specific measurement device that will be used to determine the degree to which performance levels are achieved

The phrases that appear next to letters A through E on the chart read as a complete sentence when combined. Together, they state a specific objective that is precise and comprehensive, yet modular, and, therefore, more easily understood. The format enables any reader to readily understand the program's goals for children and the degree to which children are expected to perform if the goals are to be met.

Performance Objective Outline

Product Objective #1	
Target population	**A** Spanish-dominant kindergarten children who pretest below the 16th percentile
Desired behavior	**B** will improve their reading- and learning-readiness skills in their dominant language
Performance level	**C** to the extent that 50 percent of the target population will posttest at or above the 24th percentile
Operational condition	**D** providing students have at least a 75 percent attendance rate
Instrument	**E** as measured by the Walker Readiness Test

Evaluation Plan	
General technique	readiness survey on an individual basis administered in dominant language
Baseline data	pretest
Sample group(s)	Spanish-dominant kindergarten students who pretested below the 16th percentile
Collection dates	September and May
Data analysis	criterion-referenced percentile

Elements of the Performance Objective

Target Population

The target-population description for each program objective should specify grade levels, span of grade levels, or age groups. In addition, the evaluator should note the language orientation of the target group (Spanish dominant, English dominant, bilingual, etc.). Finally, it is a good idea for this section of the chart to include a prescore, so that the evaluation is stratified and diagnostic. No matter how specific the target-population description is, the evaluation will be less diagnostic if the evaluator groups or clusters students by grade level only and discusses group-average scores. If the evaluator instead writes specific objectives for various levels of pretest performance — for example, "children who pretest below the 16th percentile" — the evaluation report can identify the degree to which a program is helpful to average, below-average, and above-average children. Quite often, the use of mean or average scores obscures the fact that a program did not serve a particular kind of student, most often the below-average or well-below-average child. This situation can be avoided by adding a pre-score range to each target population. For example, the following phrases describe two target populations within a kindergarten program; specific objectives and performance levels should be developed for each group. (Note: The term "Spanish-dominant" can be used interchangeably with "limited English proficiency," depending on a program's philosophy.)

☐ Spanish-dominant kindergarten children who pretest between the 15th and 30th percentiles

☐ Spanish-dominant kindergarten children who pretest at or below the 15th percentile

Other descriptors of a target population could include number of years in the United States, number of years in a bilingual-education program, or any other factors that are relevant to student growth.

At times, the cutoff points for identifying subgroups within an objective are not known until after pretesting is completed. If historical data on which to base these groupings and expectancies are not available, the evaluator can prepare a comprehensive objective and delineate groupings at a later date.

Desired Behavior

After identifying and grouping the target population, the evaluators and teachers can then generally state the instructional area that the objective is to address. Examples are "will improve reading comprehension," "will improve math computation skills," or "will improve oral language capabilities."

Performance Level

Next the design format requires a specific description of the required performance level. These criteria are often dependent on the overall research model. For example, if appropriate comparison groups are available, the notation here would refer to the intergroup comparisons. A sample performance level based on intergroup comparisons might read: "to the degree that the bilingual students score at least 10 points higher than the comparison-group children." A performance level using intergroup comparisons may be based on inferential statistics (degree of significance in the difference between two groups), increased gain scores (mean grade equivalencies, percentiles, raw scores), or a reduction in the gap between the two groups if the bilingual program group is behind the comparison group at the beginning of the year.

The performance-level section of an objective is a criterion for success and may also be a direct reflection of the overall research model. For example, if inferential statistics are being utilized, the performance level would mention a probability level at which significance would be accepted ($p = .05$). If the research design is based on a skill approach to growth, the performance level would cite the criterion-referenced growth rate or the manner in which a specific skill would be demonstrated. An example of a criterion-referenced performance level would be "to the degree that 50 percent of the limited English-speaking children will obtain reading readiness scores at or above the 35th percentile rank."

Operational Condition

The operational condition of an objective tells what must take place in order for the instructional activities to be held accountable. For example, it would be unfair and unrealistic to hold a teacher or instructional program responsible for growth among youngsters who have attendance rates below 50 percent. In this instance, counselors and supportive services must work to increase attendance. Similarly, a teacher cannot be held accountable for academic growth if he or she needs to provide small-group instruction but is not given appropriate materials or the assistance of a teacher aide. In this case, the operational condition might read: "providing the teacher is given the services of a teacher aide by November 1." The operational condition should not be considered a "cop-out" on the part of the program or the teacher. Rather, it is part of a two-way accountability model. If the teachers and instructional activities are to be held accountable, so too should administrators and supportive services.

The operational condition also makes evaluation more diagnostic. When an evaluator is about to examine a set of pre-post data, he or she should first look at the operational condition in order to eliminate certain students or even an entire objective. For example, suppose the operational condition states that a teacher aide is essential to the achievement of a particular goal. If the evaluator discovers that an aide was not provided until April or May, he or she immediately knows that there will be a problem with the data and can offer diagnostic input. If a particular operational condition relates to attendance, the evaluator first reviews attendance rates and eliminates students who are below the prescribed level in certain evaluation studies. Of course, the evaluator should also examine the growth rate of all children in the program, regardless of attendance. In this way, the evaluator can test the validity of the operational condition. If there is no difference between growth rates for the entire target population, the operational condition is inappropriate.

Instrument

The last part of an objective indicates an instrument to be used in collecting measurement data. If the instrument is made part of the stated objective, program developers are less likely to postpone instrument selection.

Evaluation Plan

The lower portion of the Performance Objective Outline describes the evaluation plan specifically related to the objective presented. This is another step toward making evaluation activities an integral part of a service-oriented bilingual-education program. As each objective is developed, the program developers and evaluators can discuss and prepare the associated evaluation plan.

The categories in this section of the chart can be defined as follows:

☐ General technique: a general indication of the data-collection activity to be used (e.g., individualized testing)

☐ Baseline data: a description of the preliminary or initial scores used as a basis for comparison or as a beginning for growth measurement

☐ Sample group(s): usually the same as the target population in the related objective; however, when sampling is done, the sample procedures or the sample group is defined here

☐ Collection dates: dates when pretest and posttest will be collected

□ Data analysis: description of plans for analyzing data
(e.g., t-test for the difference in means)

Process Objectives

After program planners develop product objectives, they may
then develop a process objective for each product objective.
Product objectives are goals that describe the growth rates of
children. Process objectives are goals that describe the educational activities aimed at bringing about the ultimate products.

Performance Objective Outline

Product Objective #2	
Target population	**A** Portuguese-dominant children in grades 3 and 4 who score below 2.0 on the math pretest
Desired behavior	**B** will acquire mid-primary conceptual development and related computation skills
Performance level	**C** as demonstrated by a growth of 1.5 grade equivalencies by 50 percent of the target population
Operational condition	**D** after being diagnosed by the math consultant with a concept-oriented battery
Instrument	**E** as measured by a standardized computations test (CTBS)

Evaluation Plan	
General technique	standardized computations test
Baseline data	pretest
Sample group(s)	all who pretest below 2.0
Collection dates	September and May
Data analysis	criterion reference: 50 percent grow 1.5 years

Performance Objective Outline

Process Objective #2	
Target population	**A** the bilingual-classroom teachers and the school system's math specialist
Desired behavior	**B** will use a concept-oriented diagnostic test to plan math activities for target students
Performance level	**C** to the extent that all grade 3 and 4 children scoring below 2.0 will be diagnosed per conceptual development
Operational condition	**D** providing project administrators purchase diagnostic battery prior to Nov. 15
Instrument	**E** as recorded on student records and evaluator's tally sheets

Evaluation Plan	
General technique	review of diagnostic records
Baseline data	N/A
Sample group(s)	bilingual-classroom teachers and the school system's math specialist
Collection dates	November
Data analysis	trend analysis: review of diagnostics

The two charts on pages 20-21 demonstrate related product and process objectives.

The product goal calls for a growth rate of 1.5 years on a standardized test of mathematics. However, the operational condition for the product objective requires that each child scoring below 2.0 on a pretest be diagnosed with a concept-oriented battery.

The process objective for this product goal directly relates to the utilization of diagnostic materials. In this instance, the use of diagnostic testing is a process essential to the achievement of the product. In deciding which process to identify as a goal, the evaluators should work closely with teachers. These two charts were taken directly from an evaluation plan developed by a group of teachers working with the author. After identifying the product objective for third- and fourth-grade youngsters who pretested below 2.0 in math computations, the teachers decided that the concept-oriented diagnostic work was the key process toward eventual achievement of the product goal. Consequently, that process became the related process goal. We will examine program processes more carefully in the next chapter.

4 Evaluating Program Processes

The evaluation of a bilingual-education program is not diagnostic unless it reviews program processes as well as products. The products of a program are the affective and cognitive gains demonstrated by participating students (see Chapter 3). The processes are techniques, methods, and materials used by the program. An evaluation limited to product-related pretesting and posttesting may have a valid research design. However, without a process review, such an evaluation is research isolated from program operations. Without assessing or monitoring a program's instructional processes, the evaluation cannot discuss student gains in a cause-and-effect fashion and cannot make specific curriculum recommendations.

Since most evaluation budgets are limited, few evaluators have the opportunity to observe classroom activities long enough or often enough to become involved in process consultations with teachers. However, when the evaluator does go into the classroom, his or her role and function should be clearly defined to preclude a situation in which the teacher views the evaluator as a supervisor.

Quantity and Quality: Preservice and In-service

In order to establish a constructive relationship, the process evaluator and teacher must first discuss role limits and role relationships. During preservice or early in-service sessions, evaluators and teachers should review program processes, evaluation philosophies, and process-evaluation data-collection activities. At that time, the teachers and evaluators should specifically identify a series of process objectives to be addressed. These goals may be expressed in two ways: quantitatively and qualitatively.

A quantitative process objective and its related evaluation procedure is relatively easy to define and nonthreatening to evaluate, as demonstrated by this example:

> Bilingual teacher aides at the kindergarten level will reinforce each day's ESL presentation by reviewing a related lesson in Spanish for 20 minutes as outlined in the Spanish-language reading-readiness curriculum guide.

In order to assess such a specifically stated, quantitative process objective, evaluators need only observe the classrooms, review the daily plans, and determine the degree to which the quantitative requirements are met. Quantitative process objectives may call for a number of lessons per day, a number of minutes devoted to a specific topic per day, a number of individualized activities, or any observably quantifiable activity. (The Performance Objective Outline discussed in Chapter 3 may also be used to develop quantitative process objectives.)

Although this approach seems overly simplistic, many programs benefit from it, especially if the product data confirm a positive relationship between student achievement and the achievement of quantitative process goals. On the other hand, a program could meet all of its quantitative process goals and still fall short of program effectiveness due to ineffectual daily processes. Thus, it is necessary to develop qualitative process objectives and corresponding evaluation activities that are designed to measure "how well" rather than simply "how much."

When evaluators begin collecting qualitative process data, they run the risk of entering into a supervisory relationship with teachers. Again, preservice and in-service activities are crucial to prevent such a situation. After evaluators and teachers agree on a set of process goals, they should participate in a series of simulation games during which evaluators demonstrate how they will gather and present qualitative information. Teachers should also be aware that they will be able to provide feedback about the evaluation team and its recommendations. Once the teachers see that evaluators can provide objective, useful information in a nonthreatening fashion, the door is open to a qualitative process evaluation.

Classroom Observations and Private Consultations

Preservice and in-service workshops can also be used to schedule brief private consultations following each classroom visit. After observing classroom activities related to the agreed-on process goals, the evaluator should set aside time for a loosely structured meeting with each teacher or aide. These discussions may address curriculum, scheduling, program management, parent involvement, and other instructional and noninstructional processes. By posing a series of open-ended questions, the evaluator gives teachers and aides an opportunity to supply input to the evaluation data bank and to provide information about future modifications of their program. All too often, the professionals and paraprofessionals who are most responsible for the regular operation of the instructional program are left out of the evaluation process. If an evaluation team visits each classroom at least twice during the school year, the teachers and aides can make major contributions to the evaluation findings.

During classroom visits, members of the evaluation team should not examine or evaluate the performances of teachers or aides. Rather, they should assess the bilingual-education instructional processes, especially those that differ from the local educational mainstream processes. Quantitatively speaking, the evaluators should identify the degree of bilingual process implementation. Qualitatively, they should assess bilingual curriculum materials, bilingual individualization, utilization of dominant-language teaching techniques, and other processes. A direct assessment of teacher performance in areas that do not affect bilingual instruction is not appropriate and should be actively guarded against.

Very few evaluators are in a classroom long enough or often enough to assess completely any teacher or teacher aide. Consequently, teaching practices should be approached on a group basis. In other words, the evaluator can use a checklist to collect qualitative process data and to identify trends among an anonymous group of teachers and aides. In this way, the resulting evaluation recommendations are pertinent yet not directed at specific individuals. A typical qualitative process evaluation statement might say: "Kindergarten teachers involved in the bilingual program need to examine the degree to which their Spanish-language reading-readiness activities are being reinforced by the ESL component." The evaluation report might then go on to discuss specific teaching practices (but not specific teachers) that the evaluator observed.

Teacher-Interview Questionnaire

Evaluators should supplement their classroom visits by draw-ing on the experiences and opinions of participating staff mem-bers. The Teacher-Interview Questionnaire (Appendix C) was designed to encourage teacher input into the program-evaluation component. The questionnaire is intentionally open-ended rather than highly structured to give teachers an opportunity to discuss program strengths and weaknesses in a free-flowing fashion. Teacher-generated data can account for as much as 50 percent of an interim report, especially if it is a process report.

The first two questions of Part I collect data on student selection, an important process to review, especially if the evaluation team wishes to examine the degree to which a pro-gram is serving the children with the greatest need. In addi-tion, student-selection processes should be studied to ensure an objective evaluation. If the students are selected according to inappropriate variables, the evaluation could be biased. For example, in one particular program, second-grade Hispanic children are required to demonstrate certain Spanish reading skills before joining a bilingual program. After the school year starts, the program stresses developmental reading skills. The evaluation of this program is necessarily skewed toward suc-cess, because the students already possess many of the skills the program emphasizes. To better serve these students, the program should expand and build on those reading skills already attained and evaluate student progress in new learning areas. Question 3 on the survey elicits information about the reading level of program participants. These first questions on student background are intentionally general; as teachers progress through the survey, they are asked to focus more spe-cifically on instructional strengths and weaknesses.

In Part II of the questionnaire, teachers describe the class-room structure or instructional model. These questions are posed for several reasons. First, it is always interesting to com-pare the perceptions of teachers with those of outside observers. For example, if a team of teachers describes its instructional setting as an open one while the outside evalua-tor perceives the classroom as a traditional model, further dis-cussion is indicated. Additionally, models have a direct effect on evaluation if they differ from one classroom to another. If one second-grade teacher has implemented an open-classroom model while another second-grade teacher in the same build-ing is working on a team model, interclass comparisons take on additional significance. Interclass comparisons on a model-by-model basis should not take place unless the teachers involved verify the fact that they are, indeed, working with specific instructional designs.

Questions 4 and 5 ask if the model being used is applicable to bilingual teaching. At first, these questions might seem inappropriate. Actually, however, evaluators frequently find teachers working with instructional models — perhaps required by local mandate or by a federally funded program — that have little or nothing to do with bilingual instruction. For example, the author once had an opportunity to evaluate a bilingual program conducted in the same buildings as a Project Follow-Through program. In this instance, the Follow-Through program was atempting to replicate the Tucson Early Education Model (TEEM). In order to comply with TEEM and to receive federal funds for this purpose, the lower-elementary-level teachers had to follow certain guidelines and regulations. Unfortunately, several of the Follow-Through processes did not conform easily to the bilingual-instructional processes. If the teachers had not been given an opportunity to comment officially on the relationship between their instructional model and bilingual instruction, the conflicts between the two might have continued undiscovered.

Question 5 focuses on team teaching. Bilingual instruction is rooted in individualized instruction, which is best defined as an approach that builds on student strengths. Team teaching is often used in individualized instruction, especially in programs that group youngsters according to student strengths within or across grade levels. Many bilingual programs are using such team-teaching models.

Part III of the Teacher-Interview Questionnaire asks teachers to identify specifically the degree of Spanish-language instruction provided to Spanish-dominant students. This is the crux of bilingual education. Spanish-dominant youngsters should receive instruction in Spanish until they are ready to begin some instruction in English. Unfortunately, many bilingual-education programs fall short of this goal. The questionnaire documents, through teacher observation, the degree to which Spanish instruction is actually provided. The questions in this phase of the survey are specific. They require the teacher to identify the subjects being taught in Spanish, the subjects being reinforced in Spanish, the available materials, and the persons responsible for instruction (teacher, aide, etc.). These questions are asked in order to collect supplementary data in some instances and preliminary data in others. If outside evaluators visit each instructional location only two or three times a year, they cannot possibly make decisions about program processes without assistance. Teacher interviews can be used to guide the evaluators. When data from these interviews are analyzed, the evaluators can direct attention to particular instructional processes for any of the following reasons:

- ☐ Lack of adherence to federal, state, or local guidelines for Spanish-language instruction
- ☐ Lack of cohesion with the local program's proposal or program design
- ☐ Conflicts between implemented processes from one room to another
- ☐ Lack of bilingual instruction

Part IV of the questionnaire deals with Spanish-as-a-second-language instruction. SSL is not mandated by bilingual-education regulations at either the federal or the state level. However, many bilingual programs have learned that bilingual education achieves greater acceptance and success if English-dominant children in a participating class are given second-language instruction in Spanish. Evaluators can use this section of the survey to elicit responses to scheduling, modalities, and materials.

The fifth part of the Teacher-Interview Questionnaire addresses instruction in English as a Second Language. Questions resemble those in Parts III and IV.

Part VI asks teachers to comment on the assignments given to paraprofessionals, specifically as regards scheduling and duties. Teachers are *not* asked to assess the aide's performance qualitatively. This information may be sought confidentially with another scale.

The last two parts of the survey focus on parent involvement and program communications. If there is an active parent component, parents usually visit the classrooms freely. If there is not an active parent component in the program, responses here will document that fact. As far as program communications are concerned, teachers are usually willing to assess honestly a bilingual-project director's capabilities. Communications are important to a bilingual-education program, since it is usually relatively new to a school system. Excellent internal communications are essential if the program is ever to gain external acceptance and acknowledgment. Answers to these questions give project directors an opportunity to objectively consider their accessibility, sensitivity, and rapport with teachers.

To analyze the data from the questionnaire, the evaluator should use a trend analysis or a critical-incident technique. In a trend analysis, the evaluator reads each of the surveys — completed by an interviewer or the teachers — and identifies programmatic strengths and weaknesses from response patterns. The critical-incident approach requires the evaluator to identify programmatic areas before reading the responses and to look only for those critical incidents in the responses. For example, if the evaluator selects the critical incident "lack of materials," he or she looks through each survey for any comments related to lack of materials. First-time evaluators should use both techniques when reviewing open-ended data of this nature.

Scheduling

Scheduling classroom visits and interviews is sometimes difficult. If an evaluator has three opportunities to visit a classroom, he or she should make an initial short visit (15–20 minutes) sometime between the opening of school and the beginning of November. During this first visit, the evaluator takes no notes and only looks quickly at the program's instructional activities. The second observation, made during midyear, may be longer (45–60 minutes) and may include the teacher interview. In this way, the evaluator is able to present process findings in an interim report submitted sometime between January 15 and February 15. During the last visit, conducted just prior to posttesting, the evaluator provides feedback based on the first two observations. However, teachers should receive evaluatory information through other channels as well (e.g., workshops).

Evaluators who supplement classroom observations with comprehensive interviews are able to provide programmatic recommendations that are useful in improving student services. Additionally, by regularly asking teachers and aides to provide information, evaluators are more likely to win the support and trust of these vital staff members.

5 Measuring Growth in Early-Childhood and Kindergarten Programs

Unfortunately, too few preschool bilingual-education programs exist. Educators, developmental psychologists, and sociologists agree that low-income and limited-English-proficiency youngsters must participate in formal educational activities before they enter regular kindergarten programs if they are expected to possess developmental and prereading skills at or near the levels of their middle-income, English-speaking classmates. Title I programs, Operation Headstart, and other educational plans account for thousands of publicly sponsored preschools throughout the nation, but less than five percent of these programs are bilingual. Considering the fact that most metropolitan areas and many rural areas include limited-English-speaking preschoolers, this low percentage represents an almost total lack of treatment.

Consequently, evaluators of kindergarten bilingual programs often discover that many youngsters have difficulty responding to basic standardized instruments for kindergarten. Test tasks that require no paper and pencil, no use of inference, and very little skills mastery are still difficult for many limited-English-speaking kindergarteners, simply because they have not had the advantage of living in a society that continuously provides developmental stimuli in their native language. As a result, traditional kindergarten instruments, even when translated and adapted, may be of little use in measuring growth. The program evaluator may need to rely on preschool tests for the kindergarten level. Regrettably, the most widely used preschool instruments are still available only in English, so some local adaptation is required.

If a school system does provide bilingual preschool education, the evaluator should measure the degree to which that program imparts preschool or age-level skills. The skills-oriented instruments administered should closely reflect the curriculum used locally on a daily basis. Once the skills are measured, they should be reviewed by the evaluator, with additional input from teachers and aides.

Criterion-Referenced Instruments

The following are examples of criterion-referenced tests currently used to evaluate preschool and kindergarten components:

☐ *Denver Developmental Screening Test*

☐ *Peabody Picture Vocabulary Test*

☐ *Vocabulary Comprehension Scale*

☐ *Kraner Preschool Math Inventory*

These tests measure basic readiness skills. All are available only in English. However, since the preschool or kindergarten child is not reading from the test booklet, the language of the manual and testing-kit materials may be translated and adapted to meet local needs. If an evaluator is responsible for translating an instrument, he or she should work with an administrator and a teacher during the initial translation. Then, a native Spanish-speaking paraprofessional, parent, or clerical assistant should review the test for comprehension. In this way, the local program ensures that the language used by educators can be understood by those with less professional training. Also, since paraprofessionals often administer individualized tests, their involvement at an early stage promotes a greater degree of standardization in the testing procedures. Of course, the most desirable arrangement is for Spanish-speaking professionals or psychometricians to administer the tests.

Readiness Instruments

If a preschool bilingual component emphasizes prereading and prelearning skills, other tests are more advisable. These instruments include the *Walker Readiness Test*, the *Boehm Test of Basic Concepts*, the *Tests of Basic Experiences (TOBE)*, the *STAR*, and the *APELL Test*.

The *Walker Readiness Test* is available in Spanish, French, and English versions. However, many bilingual programs find the Spanish directions inappropriate for the suggested age/ grade levels. Changing the directions is simple and does not mean that local teachers are changing the test even moderately. At most, synonyms for difficult words are used. The test has 50 items and takes approximately 15 minutes to administer on an individual basis. Testers can also work with two or three youngsters at a sitting, increasing the time required to approximately 30 minutes. However, the net time savings, approximately 15 minutes, is not worth the loss of total objectivity. The *Walker Readiness Test* has subtests in four areas: similarities-differences, largest-smallest, number recognition, and missing parts. Several drawings are in need of revision, and some of the largest-smallest items are confusing in that the choices are not significantly different. Such flaws result in random responses, but these shortcomings can be rectified on a local level. The test booklets are reusable, since each child's responses are recorded on a separate answer sheet.

The *Boehm Test of Basic Concepts* is simple, straightforward, and also available in Spanish. Each of the two forms consists of 50 pictorial items arranged in approximate order of increasing difficulty. The items for each form are presented in two booklets of 25 test questions each. Each item is a set of pictures; the examiner reads statements about the pictures to the children and instructs them to mark the picture that illustrates the concept being tested. Each booklet requires approximately 15–20 minutes to administer on a group basis; the test may also be given individually. The manual prepared by this test's developer is one of the better ones on the market. The script is useful and appropriate to the needs of the test administrator and the children. A class-record form serves as a scoring key and an interpretive aid to the teacher. This test and the associated record-keeping devices give the bilingual preschool or kindergarten teacher an opportunity to identify individual children whose overall levels of concept mastery are low, as well as those individual concepts that large numbers of children find unfamiliar.

Although used by many preschool programs, the *Tests of Basic Experiences (TOBE)* are more appropriate for kindergarten and first grade. Since this instrument does provide feedback related to student skills in mathematics, language, science, social studies, and general concepts, it can be especially useful to bilingual programs conducting longitudinal studies or attempting to eliminate instructional weaknesses throughout an elementary-school program. This test is more useful for instructional guidance than for classifying children into categories. It is especially appropriate if a bilingual program is individualized in nature and starts youngsters at different points along a curriculum continuum. The *TOBE* may be given to a group or to individuals.

The *STAR* is also diagnostic in that it identifies skills strengths and weaknesses, but it does so in a manner that allows the teacher to make generalizations about concept development. The *STAR* has one feature not shared by the other three tests described: a checklist completed by the teacher. All the other tests are completed entirely by the student. The *STAR* permits the teacher to draw inferences from direct observation. This combination of teacher and student participation is sometimes useful. For example, even if a student does not respond at all to certain test items, the teacher may still conclude that development actually has taken place in the area being tested.

Another instrument that may prove useful in program evaluation is the *APELL Test*. This battery comprehensively measures entry-level development in prereading, premath, and language in order to identify deficiencies that may obstruct future learning. If used appropriately, it can also provide the basis for developing instructional strategies and assessing individual progress. The publisher provides test booklets, tally sheets, individual computer scoring cards for students, a teacher's manual in English and Spanish, and a comprehensive manual that assists in the development of instructional strategies. Computer scoring services are available. The test measures similarities, number concepts, use of pronouns and verbs, visual discrimination, and several other areas of instruction. The manual is unique in that it specifically identifies testing areas and relates each testing area to program performance objectives and to various test items.

If the suggestions provided in the manuals for these tests are not followed, the normative data are sometimes rendered irrelevant. However, this does not mean that the instruments are useless for bilingual preschool or kindergarten evaluation. If there are no modifications made in the test, any of these instruments can be used for pretesting and posttesting without the norm scores and conversions. Raw scores from these tests, with comparison groups or inferential statistics, are an appropriate measure of growth from beginning to end of year.

At the kindergarten level, the same tests can be used. All of the instruments have age-based norms that permit the test to be used over a wide age range. For example, the *Walker Readiness Test* can be used with ages four through seven. However, each six-month growth in chronological age requires a greater number of correct responses for maintenance of initial percentile rank. This characteristic makes the *Walker Test* a more legitimate pre-post measurement device than most tests, especially those that do not have age-based percentiles.

At the kindergarten level, local decisions regarding the teaching of prereading skills should affect the degree to which prereading tests are used in an evaluation. For example, certain standardized instruments measure acquisition of such finite skills as letter names, letter sounds, and matching. These tests make for interesting evaluation designs, especially when different proficiency levels are included within the program. Non-English-speaking children who are learning to read in their native tongue would constitute one group, youngsters who have bilingual oral skills and are being taught to read with English developmental skills would make up another, and English-dominant youngsters would be a third group. By analyzing data from these groups and an external comparison group, the evaluators can determine the program's impact on the various language backgrounds.

The author has successfully used the Stanford Early School Achievement Test (SESAT) to evaluate program impact at the kindergarten level in Los Angeles and other cities. The test is available in English and Spanish with separate manuals for Puerto Rican and Mexican children. It has sub-test scores related to science and social studies (the environment), language, and other areas. Although the author's team felt that some SESAT items were culturally biased (e.g. What does a bear do in winter?), the test results can be used to examine the curricular needs of a program. The evaluator should first ensure that pre-test scores do not become part of a student's record. After administering the test, the evaluator should analyze the results to determine those topics that need to be reviewed in a more comprehensive manner because the related knowledge may not be part of a linguistic minority child's information bank (e.g. bears hibernating).

Cultural Fairness

Unfortunately, nearly all the tests discussed in this chapter were initially or primarily prepared in English. Different regions of the country may find different items culturally unfair. However, in a national survey about instruments (see Chapter 16), not one bilingual program commented that any of these tests were culturally unfair. Some programs did identify one or two items on particular tests that were inappropriate to their populations, but they did not feel that the inclusion of these items was an upsetting experience for the children. Furthermore, these one or two items did not affect the child's score to the extent that the program or the child would be grossly underrated or unfairly evaluated.

6 Measuring Growth in Oral Language

The greatest debates among bilingual educators center around oral language development and related testing:

- ☐ Is a child's oral language development as important as (or more important than) reading development?
- ☐ Should oral language skills be used to identify a child's dominant language?
- ☐ Should an assessment of oral language be based on receptive language abilities or productive language abilities?
- ☐ Should reading skills development and oral language development be related in a program?
- ☐ Should a program emphasize oral language development in Spanish, oral language development in English, or both?
- ☐ Can there be parallel oral language development in two languages?

These and many more questions arise when a local program attempts to design evaluation activities related to oral language development. Until that time, these debates, if they do take place, occur on a philosophical rather than a practical level. Unfortunately, while oral language measurement is among the most important processes in a bilingual evaluation design, it is also the most difficult. Foremost among the difficulties is the fact that language as a symbolic and generative process does not lend itself to formal assessment. In addition, measurement of productive language must be conducted on an individualized basis. And, if a local program bases its assessment of oral language development only on receptive oral skills, is oral language really being measured?

Receptive Vocabulary Instruments

Since the late sixties, many programs have relied on the *Inter-American Series: Comprehension of Oral Vocabulary* and very few other instruments designed to measure oral vocabulary. The *Inter-American* calls for the student to identify a picture that represents the words spoken by the test administrator; the child is never asked to speak. Tests like the *Inter-American* measure receptive vocabulary. By some accounts, if a child were given a receptive vocabulary test in English and a receptive vocabulary test in Spanish, the teacher could identify the child's dominant language. But receptive instruments are very limited and can have negative results: a teacher may conclude that a child is to receive instruction in a particular language without ever actually perceiving the child's total ability to conceptualize or to process thoughts and information.

Unlike receptive instruments, productive vocabulary tests call for the child to respond verbally after seeing a picture or hearing a verbal stimulus. Most programs feel that oral language development should be measured with productive language skills. This does not mean that programs should discontinue receptive measurements; however, a child's dominant language should not be determined on the basis of receptive vocabulary alone.

Defining Language Dominance

Before going further, it might be wise to review some of the more common definitions of the term *dominant language:*

- ☐ Language of the home: This definition is somewhat weak in that data often tend to be unreliable.

- ☐ Social or playground language: This definition can be misleading. Many children pick up playground English (e.g., "Gimme that ball") before they acquire English skills suitable for survival in an instructional setting.

- ☐ Language proficiency: Different from language dominance, proficiency represents the strengths a child has in a given language. A child may be proficient to a certain degree in English but still be Spanish dominant.

☐ Instructional language: In the opinion of many, the language in which a child can best receive and understand instruction is the child's dominant language.

In order to identify instructional language, one must require not only the production of language but also the production of language in response to a structured presentation rather than a simple word. Several instruments do present youngsters with sentences and directions to which they must respond. By demonstrating understanding and by providing reasonable and useful responses, the students are able to convey their potential to respond to instruction.

Types of Tests

To date, the most popular approaches for measuring oral language include interviews, storytelling, question-and-answer sessions, and language repetition or completion. In addition to using one of these four major approaches, tests usually fall into one of the four categories of language usage:

☐ Vocabulary tests: require students to select one or two words in response to a stimulus

☐ Phonology tests: measure the degree to which children recognize or use specific sound features of a language

☐ Grammar/syntax tests: sometimes labeled "fluency" tests; usually require children to arrange and use words or units of a sentence appropriately

☐ Semantics tests: require children to express or demonstrate concept understanding through language; used at the elementary level more than at the secondary level

Programs can use the major approaches and the four types of language usage to establish language-development goals; to develop procedures that promote first-language maintenance and second-language acquisition; and to evolve working definitions for key terms such as bilingual education, second-language instruction, dominant language, receptive oral vocabulary, and productive oral vocabulary.

Recent Tests in Use

The *Basic Inventory of Natural Language* (*BINL*) is a highly successful, multifaceted approach to measuring natural language development. It measures growth in various domains and skill areas and is recommended by many experienced bilingual educators. Programs using this instrument report its success as a student selection tool, a language-dominance identifier, and a program-evaluation tool. Its strength lies in the fact that it integrates various language arts and does not identify a child's dominant language on the basis of any one skill. On the other hand, the *BINL* is rather lengthy and cumbersome to administer, especially for paraprofessionals. Despite these weaknesses, many bilingual educators feel that the results and applicability of results are well worth the time and energy expended in administration.

The *Bilingual Syntax Measure (BSM)* has become the most widely used instrument in bilingual education. Just as some instruments are too broad in their language-dominance criteria, the *BSM* has been characterized as too limited. It scores only morphemes, and many researchers question how meaningful such limited results are as a measure of productive and receptive language ability. The test comes in kit form, is quite easy to administer, and can be completed in less than fifteen minutes. It is recommended by the publishers for use in grades K–2, but many evaluators, including the author, have used the instrument successfully at grades 3–5. Degree of success is sometimes dependent on the rapport between the administrator and the student. *BSMII* gives the program an opportunity to test students a few years older.

The *BSM* is commercially available in Spanish and English; different programs and school systems are in the process of developing Italian, French, and Portuguese versions, all with the permission of the publisher. However, the initial kit is needed in order to use these locally produced editions. Information regarding other language versions is available from the publisher. The scoring system has recently been criticized for being less than totally standardized.

In the *John T. Dailey Language Facility Test*, the child is asked to describe three large photographs. The instrument is an individually administered, oral productive vocabulary test. The child's language is recorded on tape or written verbatim by the test administrator. Each child's score is based on ability to use appropriate phrasing, sentence structure, creativity, and vocabulary. A rating sheet considers nine criteria, including syntax, relationships between objects, people and occurrences in the pictures, length of sentence, and number of sentences. The test has two strong points: first, the child actually produces language and, second, the test rates the child on several different criteria. However, the *John T. Dailey* intermingles various criteria without attaching weights or priorities. For example, if a child describes a photograph using a single word (e.g., "boy"), he or she receives a score of 1. If the child describes the same picture by saying "a nice boy," he or she receives 2 points. Because of the test's scoring difficulties, rater reliability may be a problem. When several raters are asked to review tapes or transcriptions of a child's response to a *Dailey* photo, they do not always concur. In order to overcome this difficulty, all tests, both pre- and post-, in a particular program should be scored by one rater.

The *Dos Amigos Verbal Language Scale* was one of the earlier bilingual language-dominance tools. According to most project reports, it is easy to administer and can be used as an initial screening device. It has been used widely with varying degrees of success. Most of the projects using *Dos Amigos* also use other instruments because they feel the test alone is too general. However, most users also add that its format allows group administration, which promotes earlier implementation of bilingual instruction. Program implementors are able to begin more quickly because the test provides an early gross measure of language skills. They then follow up the *Dos Amigos* data collection with a more refined or diagnostic instrument.

The *Spanish-English Dominance Assessment Scale* includes five separate components: a description and specification of forms, scoring forms, instruction and scripts for interviewers, instructions for the recorder, and a specifically defined letter for use with teachers during validation. In information provided to this author, the developers noted that the instrument should be "modified to suit local conditions [author's note: allow for dialectal or sociolinguistic differences] and validated locally." In brief, the assessment is primarily useful with first- and second-grade children and is helpful in identifying dominant language and, therefore, language of instruction. While other instruments use syntax as their primary approach to identifying dominant language, this instrument states that "vocabulary fluency is a good measure of knowledge of a language." Although the instrument uses tape recordings, the recordings are not necessary for initial classification of dominance. They can be used when dominance scores are doubtful. The instrument is based on descriptions of situations. For example, "Imagine you are at home in your kitchen. Tell me things you see. . . ."

The *James Language Dominance Test* requires students to respond in English or Spanish to commands about specific pictures. It has received mixed reviews among bilingual educators, primarily because of its simplicity. While other instruments are sometimes burdensome in syntactic detail, the *James Test* may err in the opposite direction. Nevertheless, hundreds of programs are relying on this instrument to identify dominant language/instructional language, to measure growth in oral language development, and to identify the relationship between growth in oral language and growth in other language arts areas. The instrument measures production of language rather than receptivity. It can be administered easily and quickly by both professionals and paraprofessionals and it is useful as a gross measure of oral language development.

According to the publishers, the *Pictorial Test of Bilingualism and Language Dominance* uses a format that appeals to children and provides a level analysis of freely elicited language samples in English and Spanish. During the test, youngsters respond to pictures. Administration and scoring can be carried out by any bilingual teacher or aide. The instrument provides four separate scores: English oral vocabulary, Spanish oral vocabulary, bilingual oral vocabulary, and total oral vocabulary. According to the developers, the test can be used to identify dominant language, children who appear bilingual but actually are not, and language-deficient children. Basically, this instrument measures oral vocabulary and language production.

The *San Bernardino Language Dominance Survey* consists of five parts and surveys comprehension in English and Spanish. It measures listening (the ability to understand and comply with stated commands), speaking (the ability to communicate with acceptable morphology and syntax), reading (the ability to comprehend sentence function by completion of fixed expressions), writing (the ability to reproduce in print simple phrases appropriate to the situation), and home language. The language of the instrument is scaled to fit four levels: K–1; primary (grades 2–4); intermediate (grades 5–6); and secondary (grades 7–12). Reliability and validity data are provided by the program that developed this instrument. It is a comprehensive survey, but one that may require slight modification by local bilingual administrators and teachers. Single copies of the entire battery, a technical manual, and forms for tallying student and group scores are available.

The *Test for Auditory Comprehension of Language (TACL)* is designed to measure a child's receptive language in English or Spanish. The test covers vocabulary, morphology, and syntax. The child responds to the examiner's oral stimuli in English or Spanish by pointing to one of three line drawings. If a program uses auditory comprehension as a language-dominance indicator, this test is an appropriate tool for identifying language of instruction.

The *Test of Oral Language Proficiency* is used to determine the English competence of non-English-speaking and limited-English-speaking students. It can be used in grades K–8 and measures vocabulary, pronunciation, and syntax. This instrument is especially helpful for projects using the oral language program produced by the same developer, since test items are based on the procedures of that program. Readers who are familiar with the late Louise Michael will appreciate the fact that this instrument is actually a continuation of her work. She designed and field tested an oral-aural diagnostic test to determine entering behaviors of non-English-speaking children at preschool and elementary levels. Major emphasis is on grammatical competence (structure); as such, the instrument should be used only if a program's philosophy concurs with this orientation. The test is individually administered and based on prompting cues that elicit responses indicating the speaker's ability to produce well-formed sentences.

Selecting and Using Instruments

Psycholinguists and theorists in bilingual education spend many hours and many pages discussing the various facets of oral language testing: phonology, morphology, syntax, and so forth. They generally agree on one essential point: there is no simple way to assess the language strengths of children. Furthermore, many children in bilingual programs code switch, using, for example, both English and Spanish in one communicative instance. Sociolinguists describe this type of exchange not as a mixture of English and Spanish, but rather as an example of a single linguistic repertoire. Most currently available instruments fail to describe the communicative competencies of bilingual children who code switch. One of the newest instruments, D'Avila's and Duncan's *Language Assessment Scale*, gives greater consideration to the more technical aspects of language cognition. It is rapidly becoming a widely used device for student selection and program evaluation.

Given these stumbling blocks, bilingual educators should realize that their language-assessment efforts are limited at best. To measure language dominance, programs must combine instruments. The *James Test* combined with the *Inter-American Series*, or the *BSM* combined with one or two other instruments, can be used to assess each child individually. The key to accurate assessment is to supplement the use of receptive instruments with some productive instruments. In this way, programs can be quite diagnostic, even if teachers lack expertise in psycholinguistics and language development. The objective is to measure fluency, a child's ability to understand a language presentation and to respond in kind. Of course, as teachers become more knowledgeable in language development through in-service education and as language instruments are improved, the evaluation team may wish to become more technical in their assessment procedures.

Oral Language as an Entry-Exit Measure for Bilingual Programs

When bilingual teachers and administrators assess the degree to which a bilingual program has benefited their students, they need to measure growth in several areas, including oral language development. In addition to using oral language as an assessment of program impact, it is also part of the entry-exit criteria of most programs. Most currently used bilingual oral-language-measurement devices focus on receptive vocabulary or grammar; thus, bilingual educators tend to be skeptical regarding the results collected with these assessment instruments. Until quite recently, however, little else has been available for establishing program entry-exit criteria and measuring oral language development.

In a survey conducted by this author among 200 directors of bilingual programs, many expressed the opinion that receptive vocabulary tests (instruments that require students to identify a pictured item after hearing a verbal stimulus or to respond verbally when given a pictured stimulus) often result in inappropriate placement of youngsters or irrelevant statements regarding curriculum and program effectiveness. Some students are prematurely mainstreamed by these tests, while others are incorrectly placed in bilingual programs. The former error is usually due to a child's being able to use English vocabulary in response to simple questions (e.g., What is this?) long before the child is able to apply the same vocabulary words in a learning situation. For example, a limited-English-speaking child may know a simple English definition for the word *window* long before he or she is able to use the word in an applied learning experience, such as using *window* to discuss a concept (seeing through something, keeping out the weather, etc.).

In addition, many teachers are wary of tests that identify dominance by measuring receptive vocabulary or grammatical usage, two language factors that, although deemed critical, are superficial or "surface-oriented" when compared to the total language process. Given that these factors are not sole and absolute indicators of student language ability, we can turn to the more recently developed instruments that focus on language as a cognitive function and use processes that attempt to answer the question: "In what language will the child best learn?"

These new cognitively based instruments employ a bilingual approach to assessing language-based learning skills. The theories of Piaget and other developmental psychologists whose research has focused on the relationship between language and cognition have contributed to their development. The instruments use the cognitive triad — receptive vocabulary/cognitive functioning/verbal response — rather than syntax or vocabulary development.

The cognitive triad replicates the academic language interactions that ordinarily take place between student and teacher. Thus, the assessment situation closely reflects anticipated practical classroom experiences and activities. The student demonstrates his or her school-oriented language skills in a way that permits student selection based on pertinent criteria. In a cognitively based language-testing situation, children are given verbal stimuli and are asked to manipulate information prior to a verbal response. For example, antonyms require cognition. Given the word *happy*, the child must understand its contained meaning, use cognitive abilities to associate it with its opposite, and provide a verbal response. If the child is given a *group* of antonym items and clusters of several other cognitive skills (sentence memory, digits reversed, etc.), the behaviors elicited are representative of the behaviors that would occur in day-to-day learning. When we give a student the opportunity to respond to such stimuli in both native and second languages, we can truly identify the strongest academic tongue (dominant language).

This writer's own cognitively based instrument, the *Language Assessment Umpire* (*L.A.U.*), Santillana Publishing, incorporates subtests that use sentence memory, synonyms, antonyms, and reversed digits. Although this new approach is quite unusual, its validity has been shown to be high, with the initial study having a rating of .94. Additional studies are now being conducted in order to establish performance levels that place children into the five *L.A.U.* categories. Educators corroborate the statistics. They point out that a child asked to repeat four numbers backwards in each of two languages will, after four or five sets of numbers, begin to show language-cognition patterns. Antonyms, synonyms, sentence repetition, and numbers reversed are all examples of the behaviors called for by cognitively based language instruments. When non- or limited-English-speaking students perform such skills in English as well as they perform them in their native language, they fall into *L.A.U.* Category C and are ready to receive most of their instruction in English.

Since the writing of this book, several other new tests have been validated. Lists of these instruments include: *Tests for Bilingual Education*, Santillana Publishing Company, Inc., New York, New York; *Evaluation Instruments for Bilingual Education: An Annotated Bibliography*, Dissemination and Assessment Center for Bilingual Education, Austin, Texas; and, *An Annotated List for Spanish Speakers* by Kenneth Buell, Educational Testing Service, Inc., Princeton, New Jersey. A comprehensive list of these instruments is also available from the Northwest Regional Education Laboratory, Seattle, Washington.

7 Evaluating Growth in Reading

One of the major goals of most elementary bilingual-education programs is growth in reading skills. Reading growth can be divided into several areas:

- ☐ Developmental reading (word-attack skills, syllabication, etc.) in Spanish
- ☐ Developmental reading in English
- ☐ Reading comprehension in Spanish
- ☐ Reading comprehension in English
- ☐ Reading vocabulary in Spanish
- ☐ Reading vocabulary in English

At first glance, it may appear easier for the evaluator to group several skills together in the assessment design. All too often, however, program evaluators cluster reading skills and thereby fail to provide bilingual-education programs with diagnostic evaluations of specific abilities. Educators are currently seeking more diagnostic programming; thus, evaluators should strive to provide more comprehensive assessment information.

Ideally, evaluators should measure growth in both English and Spanish reading. Under less-than-ideal circumstances, they should at least measure reading growth in each child's primary language. In other words, first- and second-grade children who are Spanish dominant should receive their initial reading instruction in Spanish, and evaluators should measure growth of these children with Spanish tests.

Tests in Use

Several reading batteries are currently available. The *Inter-American Series: Tests of Reading* are the most widely used and are among the more refined bilingual batteries. These instruments use a standard American approach, with one section for reading vocabulary and another for reading comprehension. The vocabulary section presents the child with a word and four pictures; the child is required to mark the picture that represents the word. In the comprehension section, two approaches are employed, one that uses paragraphs and pictorial stimuli and another that uses paragraphs and printed stimuli.

When the *Inter-American* tests were first released, several errors adversely affected their use in bilingual classrooms. These errors, many of which related to translation rather than adaptation, have since been eliminated on subsequent test forms. In other words, a program evaluator can now administer a Spanish *Inter-American* reading test and an English *Inter-American* reading test that are equal in difficulty although not exact translations. The buyer should review samples from the publisher to ensure that he or she is purchasing the appropriate test forms.

At this time, there are very few diagnostic reading tests available in Spanish. Although several publishers are considering adapting nationally known tests for Spanish publication, no firm commitments have been made. Evaluators who want to conduct diagnostic testing in Spanish often use nonsense words — i.e., letter combinations that are not words in any language — in the fashion of well-known diagnostic instruments, such as the *Gates-McKillop* and the *Diagnostic Reading Scales*. Reading teachers working with youngsters who need remedial assistance would also do well to utilize a nonsense-word approach to determine each child's specific needs.

Most of the reading tests in Santillana's *Reading in Two Languages* are geared toward the accompanying reading materials; however, the series does include mastery tests. In general, teachers and reading specialists find the materials useful for placement and for monitoring student progress as well as the transferability of skills from Spanish to English. Program evaluators may use inferential statistics or the mastery levels assigned to each level.

Criterion-referenced reading tests can take several forms. The most useful type measures specifically stated skills (e.g., final consonant recognition). Although most criterion-referenced reading tests are in developmental reading, teachers can also find or develop comprehension tests that are criterion-referenced. The *Comprehensive Test of Basic Skills* (*CTBS*) is an example of such a test; all the items have been analyzed and assigned to certain skill areas. The *CTBS* computer scoring prints out a criterion-referenced assessment of each child's abilities. The test is now available in Spanish. Programs can use the *Inter-American* or any other Spanish reading-comprehension test in a criterion-referenced manner if they categorize and analyze the items by areas of reading comprehension (e.g., finding the main idea.)

SOBER (*System for Objectives-Based Evaluation of Reading*) assesses reading achievement and can be used to evaluate instructional programs in reading. The program presents 200 specifically identified goals; each bilingual program chooses those goals that are most appropriate to their own local curriculum guides. *SOBER* is not normative in approach and therefore may not provide program evaluators with all they need for a comprehensive evaluation model. However, these goals and the criterion-referenced approach to evaluation are a useful supplement to a more standardized evaluation.

Over the years, the Department of Instruction of Puerto Rico has developed an extensive series of Spanish language tests, most of which measure Spanish reading. Many observers, including this author, believe that the Puerto Rican Spanish reading tests should be emulated by publishers in the United States. The tests are not directly applicable, because the normative data are based on island children, most of whom speak Spanish as their first and major language. Consequently, it is difficult to evaluate the Spanish reading progress of United States children on the basis of these norms. Local norms can be developed, however, and cities can cooperate to develop regional norms.

Translations and Regional Spanish

Most bilingual educators recognize that translations are not usually useful in program evaluation because their level of difficulty often differs from that of the original test. When adapting a test from one language into another, the adapters must ensure that the second test is based on concepts or words of equal significance and difficulty. A literal translation usually is not sufficient.

The developers of the *Inter-American* test and the Puerto Rican Spanish reading tests have eliminated translation problems in their bilingual reading batteries. However, these tests do sometimes require the elimination or revision of certain words and phrases. When using the *Inter-American* in the Northeast, program evaluators should let the bilingual staff review the test and make any vocabulary changes appropriate to the student population. Differences between Mexican American vocabulary and Puerto Rican vocabulary can frustrate examinees and result in inappropriate responses. When using the Puerto Rican battery in the Southwest, program evaluators should have the tests reviewed by their Mexican American colleagues or bilingual-program staff members.

These vocabulary problems are minor. In fact, many programs choose to ignore the one or two culturally different words and administer the test as is. Those who do modify an item or two are not jeopardizing the objectivity of their data bank; in most instances, the normative data points are inappropriate. Furthermore, many bilingual educators are fostering the notion of a general or standard American Spanish. Throughout the United States, English dialects and vocabulary differ from one location to another. English language books and tests contain words that are not common to all parts of the nation, and English speakers accept the variations with little difficulty. The same can be said for Spanish in the United States. Although individual terms and some usages differ, Spanish speakers are still able to communicate effectively with one another. Although evaluators should be aware of regional differences in language, they should not overestimate their significance.

Reading and Program Evaluation

There are several reasons for evaluating growth in reading. Most important is the need to identify each child's appropriate language for reading instruction. While it is not the sole responsibility of the evaluator to identify language dominance, reading tests are often used as an important point of reference. Often, Spanish and English reading batteries reveal that many bilingual-program youngsters do not have a true dominant reading language: they experience difficulties with both. Evaluators and teachers who recognize this go further with their testing program in order to identify reasons for poor reading skills. This necessitates diagnostic testing. Whatever tests are used, the following components should always be included when measuring reading:

☐ Testing in two languages

☐ Testing in several skills, not only comprehension

☐ Using diagnostic tests for children who are at remedial levels

☐ Providing information about subtests and test results to teachers as soon as possible

Reading in two languages is an essential part of a bilingual program; consequently, it should be evaluated carefully and thoroughly.

8 Evaluating Growth in the Affective Domain

When the federal government began its support of bilingual education, one of the stated reasons for funding this "radical" process was to improve the self-concepts of participating children and to promote more positive attitudes toward education. Consequently, most bilingual-education programs strive to improve:

- □ Self-concept
- □ Attitude toward learning a second language
- □ Attitude toward education
- □ Attitude toward bilingual education

These goals are aimed at all children involved in bilingual instruction, regardless of dominant language. Whenever possible, therefore, program evaluators should take steps to measure growth in any or all of these areas.

Three Methodologies for Measuring Self-Concept

Most evaluators do attempt to measure student growth in self-concept, using one of three possible methodologies: student interview, student response to survey, or teacher inference. Each of these approaches has identifiable weaknesses. First, who has the time to personally interview each child? If a student self-concept interview is to be at all meaningful, it should last at least five minutes. A 30-second encounter with a stranger called "the evaluator" is bound to be unproductive. In addition, the student interview puts children in an awkward situation, especially if the interview is conducted by the classroom teacher or the teacher aide. In this potentially threatening situation, the child may choose to provide survival answers — i.e., responses that will please the classroom teacher — rather than truthful answers.

The second way to collect self-concept data is to have students respond to a paper-and-pencil survey. This method requires that children be able to read at a certain grade level (a level that differs with each instrument) and to understand the questionnaires, most of which are in English. Group administration of self-concept surveys sometimes results in peer-pressure responses. Children will often respond to items in certain ways in order to avoid teasing. If they answer a question honestly, they may hear, "Look at what Juan put for number 3. He's so dumb. . . ."

The third approach asks teachers to describe their perceptions of certain behaviors and self-concepts. Scales of this nature, commonly referred to as teacher-inference scales, place heavy time demands on staff members. In addition, the evaluation schedule must be adjusted to accommodate problems related to inference usage. If a teacher completes an inference scale about a group of children too early in the school year, there is a good chance that no growth will be observed over a year's time. This is primarily due to the fact that the teacher is rating the youngsters based on their behaviors and attitudes during the first few weeks of school, before they feel socially comfortable in the new classroom environment. Only after they feel at ease will children begin to act out their problems and emotional strengths and weaknesses. Although evaluation designs call for testing during the early weeks of the academic year, evaluators should delay collection of self-concept data until mid-November if they are depending on teacher inference.

Inferential scales put no emotional stress on children, because the youngsters do not have to talk about problems with a stranger or with a classroom authority figure. In addition, teacher-inference scales eliminate peer pressure. Unfortunately, inferential scales *are* inferences rather than student-generated information. They require that the teacher observe and analyze behaviors and attitudes, and then interpret these as being representative of varying degrees of self-concept. The level of subjectivity is thus unavoidably high.

Instruments in Use

Several popular self-concept and attitude scales have been designed for certain population groups. The *Primary Self-Concept Inventory*, *School Attitude Tests* (oral and written versions), *Cultural Attitude Scales*, and *Cultural Attitude Inventories* are aimed at the Hispanic groups currently involved in bilingual education.

Among the more widely used inferential scales is *McDaniel's Inferred Self-Concept Scale.* Unlike most inferential scales, the *McDaniel's* specifically states and describes behaviors. For example, a more general instrument might say: "Student is happy about being in school." The *McDaniel's Scale* presents an item and then describes certain behaviors that exemplify happiness in school. This specificity allows for standardization from one teacher to another.

Of particular importance are those scales that address self-concept as a learner or as a student. One of the most common problems in bilingual education is that many limited-English-speaking children fail to see themselves as having academic potential. Thus, bilingual-education programs should strive to instill a sense of academic pride among children. Certain instruments can measure the degree of success in this endeavor. The *Piers-Harris Children's Self-Concept Scale* is a student-completed questionnaire that requires an English reading level of approximately fourth grade. Its format permits programs to pull out items specifically identified as predictors of self-concept as a learner.

The *Geist Picture Interest Inventory* is useful to programs wishing to measure individual or group change in interest. It is primarily aimed at males. The kit contains interest booklets, response sheets, and appropriate tally sheets. Prior to purchase, local programs should consider whether or not they wish to use measures limited by sex to evaluate their program's impact.

The *IMAR Bilingual Attitude Scale*, a brief instrument, uses a Likert approach: agree very much, agree some, disagree some, and disagree very much. One part of the scale, designed to collect data from Anglo children, begins: "There are children in your school or neighborhood that you call Spanish. Your answers to the following statements will help us to understand the way you feel about Spanish children and their language." Marleaux has developed two different approaches, one for children who are able to read and another for youngsters who need visual cues (smiling faces and frowning faces, etc.).

Two final instruments deserve mention. The *Self-Esteem Inventory*, an instrument that was recently revised to include a secondary-level survey, is available in Spanish and English and has been used to assess growth in self-concept among groups of students. Finally, the *Survey of Study Habits and Attitudes* directly addresses study and educational attitudes. Unfortunately, this instrument is available only in English.

Measuring the Self-Concept of Ethnic Minorities

Questions of self-identity, self-worth, and self-concept are socioculturally based. Often what constitutes a positive self-image in the home and community differs from the school's conception of a positive self-concept. Program evaluators should be aware of the limitations of instruments normed on populations dissimilar from the program population. Furthermore, it is pointless to translate a self-concept instrument if that instrument does not reflect the values on which self-concept in the particular ethnic culture is based.

In addition to utilizing various approaches and instruments, a local program evaluator may choose to use social indicators to measure growth of self-concept on a group basis. The social indicators must be identified by teachers and aides. In an early meeting with bilingual-program staff members, the evaluator should ask the following questions:

☐ How does the bilingual-program child demonstrate a strong self-concept, especially as a learner?

☐ How does the bilingual-program child demonstrate a weak self-concept?

☐ Which of these behaviors are objectively observable?

After a group of teachers identifies specifically observable behaviors, they can establish priorities for these behaviors and list three or four that reflect poor self-concepts and three or four that reflect strong self-concepts. The evaluator can then develop a process by which teachers periodically tally or describe the degree to which such behaviors occur. Hopefully, between the beginning and the end of the academic year, indicators of strong self-concept will increase while indicators of poor self-concept decrease.

Social indicators can be either sophisticated or simple. Here are some examples:

- [ ] Beginning learning activities on one's own after completing assigned tasks

- [ ] Perseverance in completing tasks that are challenging rather than easily accomplished

- [ ] Mingling with youngsters during free-play periods

Opposite behaviors would indicate low self-image as a learner. Each group of teachers identifies its own behaviors, many of which are directly related to instructional model, curriculum package, or other local processes.

A Sociometric Technique

During the forties and fifties, sociometry was a widely practiced science. Classroom teachers, building administrators, and educational researchers administered sociograms on a regular basis. The techniques provided teachers with feedback about sociometric choices and advised them about cliques, isolates, and group trends. During the sixties and early seventies, sociometry went out of style. Unfortunately, one of the reasons for its demise was the fact that sociometric data-collection activities became far more sophisticated then data-analysis techniques. Although evaluators were able to collect more and more data with techniques that were less obstrusive and more relevant, they could not analyze the data without hours and hours of work. Computer graphics provided an answer to the time dilemma; however, this is usually beyond the realm of most program budgets.

The current state of the art is not much more encouraging. The author and his evaluation team have developed data-collection activities that are suitable in a bilingual setting and provide teachers with data related to program impact on sociometric/ethnic choice. However, at the present time, no school systems or funding agencies have invested in the development of an appropriate computer program for analyzing the data. As a consequence, evaluators must spend approximately three hours analyzing each classroom measured with the data-collection activities described in the following pages. It is suggested that this technique be done on a sampling basis: one class per grade level in programs serving grades K–2. Above the second grade, this process seems to be less reliable.

The basic data-collection process is simple. The children's desks are arranged in a circle and each child is given a headband with a large number on the front. The group then plays any game that helps the children learn numbers. Next the evaluator distributes pencils and response sheets (Appendix D) and asks the classroom teacher to make a list identifying the children by number and ethnic group. Wearing a headband, the evaluator sits in the middle of the circle and tells the children, "Put your finger in the air; now bring it down in the box just under the happy face." The evaluation assistant should check to be sure that each child has identified the appropriate box. Then the evaluator says, "In that box write the number of the person you would like to go to the movies with." After making sure that each child has written the number of one of the children in the group, the evaluator says, "Put your finger in the air; now bring it down in the box just under the sad face. Now look around the room and write the numbers of two people you would *not* like to go to the movies with."

After the evaluation team is certain that all the youngsters know how to follow the directions of the "game," the actual data collection begins. The evaluator says, "Put your finger in the air; now bring it down in the box under the happy face with an A in it." Again, the evaluation team moves around the room to check responses. "Now look around the room and write the numbers of two people you would like to play with . . . . Write the numbers of two people you would not like to play with. . . . Write the numbers of two people you would like to do school work with. . . . Write the numbers of two people you would not like to do school work with. . . . Write the numbers of two people you would like to sit with. . . . Write the numbers of two people you would not like to sit with. . . . Write the number of the person you would like to have as a leader of the class if the teacher were going to leave the room for a few minutes."

Many educators and social psychologists oppose using negative questions in sociometric questionnaires. However, statisticians and researchers have shown that sociometry is a valid evaluation process only if positive and negative questions are used. If the games are played in a friendly rather than hostile atmosphere, the negative questions will not become as important as those that are expressed positively. Furthermore, the game concludes with a positive question, leaving the youngsters with positive statements to discuss.

Sociometric data can be analyzed in several fashions. Yule's Q is a little-known statistical process that is appropriate for analyzing sociometric data. Chi square analyses, t-tests, and other inferential statistics can also be used, depending on programmatic needs and evaluation-team capabilities. If the data are to be most helpful to teachers, they should be shown graphically. Figures 8.1 through 8.5 present examples of sociometric feedback.

Positive

Lead	3		1 1 1 2 6 1 7	2 1 1 2 1		1 5 2 1 2 3 1 1
Sit		1 2 3 2 2 2 1 4	2		4 6		1 1 1 3 4 3 2
Work	2 3 2 1 1 2 3 2 4	3 3 1 3 2		2 1 3		1 3 2 1
Play	1 1	2 2	4 1 5	2 2 1 3 5 1 2		5 2 2 3 2
Subjects	1 2 3 4 5 6 7 8 9 10 11 12 13 14 15 16 17 18 19 20 21 22 23

Negative

Not Play	1 3 1 3 2 4 3	1 5 1 2 1 1 1 3 1 2 3 1 4 1 2
Not Work	3	1 4 3 2 3 1	3 2 4 2	1 3	3 4 5 1	1
Not Sit	2	1	3 2 1 1	4 1 3 1 3 4 2 2 4 3 2 4 3

Fig. 8.1 *Summary of children chosen in positive and negative social-situation preference game*

Chosen

			PR								B								GR	BR
			F						**M**		**F**			**M**					**F**	
			3	5	15	18	22	24	6	16	4	21	23	1	2	7	17	19	8	20
PR	**F**	3	o	x	o	x	o	o	o	o	o	o	o	o	o	o	o	o	o	o
		5	x	o	o	o	o	o	o	o	o	o	o	o	o	o	o	o	o	x
		15	o	o	o	o	o	x	o	o	o	o	x	o	o	o	o	o	o	o
		18	x	o	o	o	o	o	o	o	o	o	o	o	o	o	o	o	o	x
		22	o	o	o	o	o	o	o	o	o	o	o	o	o	o	x	o	o	o
		24	x	o	o	o	o	o	o	o	o	o	o	o	o	o	o	o	x	o
	M	6	o	o	o	o	o	o	o	o	o	o	o	o	o	x	x	o	o	o
		16	o	o	o	x	o	o	x	o	o	o	o	o	o	o	o	o	o	o
B	**F**	4	o	o	o	o	o	x	o	o	o	x	o	o	o	o	o	o	o	o
		21	o	o	o	o	o	o	o	o	o	o	x	o	o	o	o	o	o	x
		23	o	o	o	x	o	o	o	o	o	o	o	o	o	o	x	o	o	o
	M	1	o	o	o	o	o	o	o	o	o	o	o	o	o	o	x	x	o	o
		2	o	o	o	o	o	o	o	o	o	o	o	o	o	o	x	x	o	o
		7	o	o	o	o	o	o	o	o	o	o	o	o	o	o	x	x	o	o
		17	o	o	o	o	o	o	o	o	o	o	o	x	x	o	o	o	o	o
		19	o	o	o	o	o	o	o	o	o	o	o	o	x	x	o	o	o	o
GR	**F**	8	o	o	o	o	o	o	o	o	o	o	o	o	x	x	o	o	o	o
BR		20	o	x	o	o	o	x	o	o	o	o	o	o	o	o	o	o	o	o
TOTALS			3	2	0	3	0	3	1	0	0	1	2	1	3	3	6	3	1	3

Fig. 8.2 *Responses to leadership question*

Chooser	Chosen					
	PR-F	PR-M	B-F	B-M	GR-F	BR-F
PR-F	6	0	1	1	1	2
PR-M	1	1	0	2	0	0
B-F	2	0	2	1	0	1
B-M	0	0	0	10	0	0
GR-F	0	0	0	2	0	0
BR-F	2	0	0	0	0	0

Fig. 8.3 *Summary matrix 1: leadership breakdown by ethnicity and sex*

Chooser	Chosen		
	PR	B	Other
PR	8	4	3
B	2	13	1
Other	2	2	0

Fig 8.4 *Summary matrix 2: leadership breakdown by ethnicity*

Chooser	Chosen	
	F	M
F	17	4
M	1	13

Fig. 8.5 *Summary matrix 3: leadership breakdown by sex*

Key		
PR: Puerto Rican	GR: Greek	M: Male
B: Black	BR: Brazilian	F: Female

Figure 8.1, although somewhat confusing at first glance, is relatively simple to use. It represents a complete summary of children chosen during a sociometric game. The students are listed numerically after the word "Subjects." By looking above and below each student's number, teachers and evaluators can tell if and how each student was chosen. For example, student 17 was selected seven times positively and only three times negatively. Interestingly, the child was chosen five times as a leader and only twice in other positive categories. Child 12, on the other hand, was picked nine times negatively and only three times positively. Such information can be useful to teachers, especially at the beginning of the school year.

Figure 8.2 is a computerized analysis of only one question: "Who would you like to have as leader of the class if the teacher were going to leave the room for a few minutes?" The "choosers" are listed vertically; the "chosen," horizontally across the top. For example, student 23, a black female, chose student 18, a Puerto Rican female, and student 17, a black male, as class leaders. The summary matrices (Figs. 8.3, 8.4, and 8.5) are also quite interesting and useful, especially if a program hopes to design and implement culturally relevant, affective learning activities.

9 Assessing Instructional-Staff Performance

The previous chapters have primarily reviewed procedures for assessing instructional activities or classroom processes and products. However, some programs may want to assess staff performance specifically. Like instructional evaluation, staff-performance evaluation relies heavily on eliciting information from participating staff members. However, it also consists of a series of activities aimed at collecting data *about* staff members rather than *from* staff members.

Unfortunately, evaluators of bilingual-education programs rarely have the necessary budget allocations and time to fairly or adequately collect data about instructional-staff members. As a result, they must rely on input from participating staff members to assess the total "process." Corroborative self-evaluation data from teachers and aides can validate other kinds of qualitative observation data. If the evaluators use anonymous self-evaluation surveys, they find that bilingual-program teachers and aides are quite honest in appraising themselves. This is especially true if the evaluator has worked to establish a constructive relationship between the evaluation team and the instructional staff.

Bilingual-Teacher Self-Evaluation Scale

Most bilingual-education programs can use the Bilingual-Teacher Self-Evaluation Scale (Appendix E). This process-evaluation tool does not and should not result in a total score or numerical rating of any teacher or group of teachers. The items are not of equal value and should not, therefore, be combined to form a score or individual rating. On the other hand, evaluators can tally this survey across items on a group basis in order to identify strengths and weaknesses among teachers.

The Bilingual-Teacher Self-Evaluation Scale contains only items that pertain specifically to the provision of instruction in a bilingual setting. As such, it primarily concerns language and is aimed at identifying strengths and weaknesses related to the teaching of language skills within a bilingual program.

A self-assessment made in good faith should be used only to structure in-service workshops. This objective is conveyed to teachers before the self-evaluation activities begin. Teachers first review the form with the evaluator during an early in-service session. They then take the form home, complete it, and mail it directly to the evaluator, with no intervention or review on the part of the principal or supervisor. The form should always be completed anonymously. After receiving all responses, the evaluator tallies them and identifies areas of strength and weakness at each grade level. Items that consistently receive lower self-ratings should be the basis for consultations and workshops. For example, if a group of bilingual teachers indicate that they are weak in teaching language skills through a multisensory approach, a learning specialist could conduct a session on the relationship of language acquisition to concept development and the use of a multisensory program for developing both areas. An evaluation team's classroom observations or survey results are always less threatening if they identify a group's training needs rather than one or two teachers' individual weaknesses.

Teacher self-evaluations should supplement rather than replace teacher and teacher-aide interviews. The Teacher-Interview Questionnaire (Appendix C) elicits information related to all facets of a bilingual-education program. It goes well beyond instructional processes and asks teachers to assess program management, curriculum, and community involvement, each of which ultimately affects the educational program. The Bilingual-Teacher Self-Evaluation Scale collects information that does not duplicate the interview data.

The first question on the self-evaluation asks teachers to identify their own language skills. Data from this item can be used for several purposes. First, it indicates if the bilingual program is adequately staffed. Second, the question identifies training needs in language skills for instructional purposes. Third, it presents terms for describing language ability. In the questionnaire, the term *transitional* refers to a person who is dominant in one language but acquiring skills in another; the person's first-language skills are stronger than the second-language skills.

The second question on the form is very important. All too often, evaluators find that programs are not providing initial reading instruction in Spanish to Spanish-dominant children. This is one of the national goals of bilingual education. Children should be taught in their dominant language, especially for developmental reading.

Many teachers and observers view bilingual education as a process that excludes English as a second language. On the contrary, those who know what bilingual education can and should do realize that dominant-language instruction and ESL form a "marriage," resulting in the *bi-* of bilingual education. The strongest programs are those in which dominant-language instruction and ESL techniques are mutually reinforcing. For example, if, on a certain day, a kindergarten teacher provides reading readiness in Spanish, developing particular concepts (e.g., above, beyond, below), the ESL lesson that day should reinforce those same concepts. This type of complementary instruction results in:

☐ Duality of purpose

☐ Reinforcement of concepts

☐ Identification of Spanish and English as essential languages

☐ Preparation for bilingualism rather than for transition into English dominance

Questions 3 and 4 on the self-evaluation scale identify the degree to which teachers provide these reinforcements. Questions 5–18 address individual training needs of teachers: items 5–15 focus on specific techniques for teaching language, while items 16–18 deal with affective issues in the classroom.

Many of the educational services provided to monolingual English classes are often overlooked or bypassed when school systems develop and implement bilingual programs. This teacher survey makes an effort to encourage the provision of remedial reading (word attack, syllabication, etc.), counseling workshops for teachers, and other processes in order to eliminate the disparity of services that often exists between bilingual and monolingual programs.

As mentioned earlier, program evaluators cannot and should not conduct comprehensive personal evaluations of participating teachers. The teachers' schedules, materials, and other activities can be evaluated by means of the teacher interview described in Chapter 4. Other processes more closely linked with teacher performance can be assessed in an anonymous fashion with the self-evaluation survey.

Evaluation of Bilingual Teacher Aides

By the same token, the evaluator should never directly assess the performance of teacher aides. He or she should, however, give the supervising or coordinating teachers an opportunity to comment on aide performance. This component of the evaluation is conducted in the same spirit as the evaluation of teacher performance. In other words, the teacher aide is assessed in order that appropriate in-service workshops can be designed to address specific weaknesses.

The evaluation form for teacher aides (Appendix F) is self-explanatory. It focuses on basic tasks, affective areas, and specific language areas. Many teacher aides do not have the education or training needed to achieve a high rating in each of these areas. Rather than designing in-service sessions haphazardly, evaluators should use teachers' comments to pinpoint areas of particular need.

10 Evaluating Curricular Materials

In the sixties, bilingual education was considered by many to be an experimental effort. Appropriate instructional materials were difficult to locate or, at times, nonexistent. Today, however, bilingual education is becoming an accepted instructional process and many major publishing houses are producing bilingual curriculum materials. Teachers are now facing a different type of problem: how to review and select materials for use in their classrooms. Primarily, teachers should assess instructional materials on the basis of locally defined needs and goals.

The Curriculum Review

The Curriculum Review (Appendix G) is one way to evaluate materials. The review is limited to ESL, SSL, and Spanish reading materials because these are the primary concerns of many bilingual programs. Each participating staff member is given a copy of the Curriculum Review and is asked to select one or two items for analysis. The local curriculum coordinator or project administrator managing the materials review should ensure that each instructional item used by the bilingual program is reviewed by more than one staff member. For example, two or three staff members should review the Spanish basal series; two or three staff members should review the ESL program; and so on.

Item 2 on the Curriculum Review asks the reviewer to identify the target group of the curriculum item. Additionally, the staff member should identify the number of children who can work with the item at any given time. Teachers and administrators need to remember that bilingual education is rooted in individualized instruction. All too often, bilingual education is looked upon as an ethnocentric approach to education. Although bilingual education developed from the commitments of various ethnic groups, it is also part of a national movement in education that began many years ago with the advent of individualized instruction. In an individualized instructional program, educators build on student strengths in order to eliminate weaknesses. What stronger tool could a child have than his or her language? Therefore, item 2 considers whether or not each material fosters individualization and permits a teacher to work with small groups or to provide instruction on an individualized basis.

The fourth and fifth questions ask teachers to assess the degree to which the curriculum item presents exercises sequentially and reinforces concepts. Unfortunately, bilingual materials are sometimes educationally unsound. This is especially true of language-arts materials that are translated literally rather than adapted. The acquisition and development of certain skills in Spanish may not follow the same sequence as in English.

If the program is to provide instruction on an individualized basis, question 6 is crucial. Students at certain grade levels should be able to work independently with Spanish materials as well as with individualized English materials.

Questions 10 and 11, which relate to horizontal and vertical relationships, are significant, since currently available bilingual materials do not span or include all possible lessons and areas of instruction. As a result, bilingual teachers often find themselves working with Spanish materials that do not coordinate well with other Spanish materials at the same level. This mismatch can be described as a poor horizontal relationship. The staff member is here asked to discuss the horizontal relationship between the reviewed item and other materials being used in the program. Can the reviewed item be used with other books? Can it reinforce other materials or be reinforced by other materials? The vertical relationship should also be examined. In other words, how well does the item relate to materials that were used before it and those that will be used after it? Frequently, bilingual programs use reading materials based on an approach (phonics, sight word, etc.) that is significantly different from the approach used in a follow-up series or in supplementary materials.

Bilingual-education teachers generally must do more lesson preparation than their nonprogram counterparts. Like all teachers, they are responsible for instruction at different levels, but they must also address different levels within different languages. For example, a bilingual teacher who is not working in a team may have to teach math in English and in Spanish at different hours. In addition, he or she may have to teach each of these math lessons at two or three different levels. Consequently, question 12 asks the reviewer to note the degree of preparation required of a teacher in order to use the materials. Bilingual teachers should be using materials that do not require extensive preparation.

Finally, the reviewer is asked if the material can be used by a teacher aide or paraprofessional. Many bilingual programs depend heavily on paraprofessional assistants for complete implementation of bilingual instruction. Unfortunately, many programs do not have the funds to train paraprofessionals fully. Therefore, staff members should choose materials that an aide can use competently without constant supervision.

Curriculum Evaluation Efforts in the United States

In the mid-seventies, the New Jersey State Department of Education contracted with the Puerto Rican Congress, a community service agency located in Trenton, to undertake a broad-ranging project related to bilingual education. One phase of the project focused on the selection and evaluation of instructional materials used in Spanish-English programs. The objective was to determine the extent to which certain products met the cognitive and affective needs of Hispanic students. After identifying a wide variety of commercial and noncommercial materials being used in New Jersey and in other states, the staff of the Puerto Rican Congress established criteria for assessing the materials. Several areas were to be examined: language, intended grade level, target group, manageability, stereotyping, program goals and objectives, specific skills, and curriculum structure. All materials were evaluated twice. First, staff members of the Puerto Rican Congress conducted a preliminary assessment; then teachers and administrators in New Jersey bilingual programs thoroughly evaluated each item. The results of these evaluations are reported in a document entitled *Evaluation Echoes*. Ninety items, including some comprehensive instructional systems, in six subject areas (English language arts, Spanish language arts, fine arts, social science, science, mathematics) are reviewed. Each review recommends how the particular product should be used, if at all.

At the same time that the Puerto Rican Congress was conducting its study, EPIE (Educational Products Information Exchange) was also examining materials used in Spanish-English instruction. EPIE, a nonprofit agency chartered by the State University of New York, gathers and distributes descriptive and analytical information about instructional materials in all areas. Its examination of bilingual-education materials was funded by the National Institute of Education. The goal of the project was to analyze the materials in a systematic fashion using *EPIEform A*, an instrument developed and continually revised by EPIE to use in its nationwide program of materials evaluation. EPIE collected over 1,200 individual instructional materials produced commercially and noncommercially both in the United States and abroad. Then a team of 36 bilingual educators, fluent in both English and Spanish and trained in the use of *EPIEform A*, examined the products. Two analysts critiqued each material and an editor synthesized their analyses, resolving discrepancies by discussion or by referral to a third analyst. *Selector's Guide for Bilingual Education Materials*, volumes 1 and 2, presents the findings of the EPIE team. Each material is identified, described, and then examined according to four "instructional design constructs": (1) rationale, goals, objectives; (2) scope and sequence; (3) methodology; and (4) means of evaluation. Manageability and bias are also considered. As in the report of the Puerto Rican Congress, each description concludes with a statement recommending if and how the material should be used.

The work of the Puerto Rican Congress and EPIE has many implications for bilingual educators. First, although such comprehensive efforts are beyond the scope of most school systems, the results of these studies are available to everyone working in bilingual education. Educators can refer to the publications of these two organizations when selecting instructional materials. Furthermore, their methods of analyzing and assessing educational products provide guidelines for teachers and administrators. Even if a particular item has not been reviewed by these two organizations, individual educators can examine the product using criteria similar to those established by EPIE or the Puerto Rican Congress. It is, of course, not wise to rely solely on the opinion of any one organization or individual when selecting materials for use in a local classroom, but EPIE and the Puerto Rican Congress certainly provide valuable assistance in making these decisions.

National Network Centers and Materials Evaluation

The U.S. Office of Bilingual Education has established the National Network of Centers for Bilingual Education. Network organizations provide a variety of services to bilingual educators, including materials development, publishing, and teacher training. Two centers in the National Network are involved in the systematic evaluation of curriculum materials. The National Assessment and Dissemination Center for Bilingual Bicultural Education, located in Cambridge, Massachusetts, has established a review procedure for tests and materials being used in bilingual programs. If a school wants information about a particular product and the Cambridge center has reviewed it, the center will provide a report that either recommends the material or pinpoints criticisms. The Dissemination and Assessment Center for Bilingual Education (DACBE), located in Austin, Texas, publishes a journal, *Cartel*, which includes critical analyses of curricular materials. Some of the areas examined are population characteristics, evidence of research and development, language level, rationale, goals, scope and sequence, methodology, and evaluation. Each analysis concludes with a summary of the product's positive and negative features.

11 Evaluating Program Management

The administrator of a bilingual-education program must grapple with several unique managerial problems. First, although most bilingual programs fall under the aegis of an existing department or school-system administrator, functionally they tend to become separate entities. Second, most educational programs involve a series of instructional activities which may or may not be supported by additional services (e.g., counseling). Many of these additional functions are ordinarily handled by noninstructional departments. For example, a local reading program concerned with upgrading developmental reading skills may also have a curriculum-development component attached to it. Bilingual-education programs almost always involve instructional components, parent-awareness activities, curriculum development, and staff-training sessions. However, few bilingual efforts have separate components or administrators for each area of concern.

Due to the complex nature of bilingual-education projects, a local director should develop a management component to coordinate the various activities and ensure implementation of the following:

☐ Curriculum-development or acquisition activities to meet specific instructional-materials needs

- [ ] Staff development, including workshops and consultations, for specific instructional weaknesses
- [ ] Community-involvement activities that meet community/parent needs and desires
- [ ] Liaison activities with other educational processes in the system and with administrators

In order to develop a comprehensive management system, evaluation activities should be considered an extension of program management. In this way, evaluation becomes a service *to* management as well as a service *of* management.

Probably at least 10 percent of the programmatic weaknesses in bilingual education are related to management rather than the instructional system. The degree to which management processes can be improved is often the degree to which a program can improve student outcomes. Program evaluators frequently see a direct relationship between poor management and lack of growth on the part of students. This is not to say that project administrators are the cause of all bilingual-program weaknesses. However, bilingual-education directors are often responsible for implementing a poor instructional model and are, therefore, responsible for lack of growth among participating children. For example, one bilingual program heavily favored a multimedia approach to language development. Many of the planned first-grade activities aimed at oral language comprehension, following directions, and oral recall required videotape recorders. Early in the school year, the teachers began reminding the project administrator about these lessons and about the fact that he had not yet ordered the videotape recorder. Several months went by, and the project administrator finally ordered the machine; unfortunately, it stayed packed in its crate in the director's office for several months following delivery. In this case, the project administrator needed to improve his management skills in curriculum development and acquisition. His inability to perform in this area had a direct impact on instructional processes and eventual student growth or lack of growth.

In the following pages, four major management functions and suggested activities are described. The evaluation team should review all of these functions and activities.

Planning

The first major management function is program and activity planning. Rather than respond to external stimuli and wait for implementation opportunities, bilingual-program directors should carefully plan the implementation of activities. Unfortunately in many school systems, bilingual education is looked on as an intrusion on the existing system. Consequently, only long-range planning fully ensures adequate implementation.

Suggested Activities

☐ *Develop comprehensive lists of expected activities.* Instead of developing a crisis-response management system, the project director should develop timelines that list specific milestones for program components. These milestones are coordinated with the program's process goals and with nonprogram activities. Each component has a separate timeline showing each week's activities. On any given Monday, a project administrator should know exactly what he or she has to do for the parent component, the training component, and so forth. These timelines become evaluation tools, since they identify dates to be met. Whenever a deadline is not met, the evaluator should identify the reasons and alter the overall evaluation plan accordingly.

☐ *Coordinate interprogram activities.* Bilingual programs often plan on a program-wide or component basis. However, they rarely plan for coordination with other programs in the school system. Since bilingual programs are so often dependent on other services (ESL, counseling, etc.) for their eventual success, interprogram coordination and communication are essential and should be an integral part of preimplementation planning.

☐ *Develop a comprehensive chronology for activities.* Timelines and coordination plans should be supplemented with a comprehensive chronological plan. After all component and interprogram plans are developed, they are collated onto a calendar. Evaluators can schedule management-evaluation activities according to the chronological plan and conduct research related to any milestones that are not met. If certain program aspects are not successful, the evaluator must determine if the chronology was inappropriate or if management has been deficient.

Acquiring and Allocating Resources

The second major management function is to acquire and allocate resources. Since bilingual education is still a new concept to thousands of school systems, school boards and key administrators are often reluctant to provide local funds and staff for a newly formed bilingual-education program. However, if a bilingual-education director wisely uses staff, materials, and monies provided by state and federal funds, a local school system is more likely to make voluntary contributions. Once local involvement has been secured, the bilingual program is well on the way to becoming an integral part of the local school district.

Bilingual programs must be particularly careful in the area of expenditures. A bilingual-education program does not generally become a permanent part of a school's budget. As a result, the administrator must work to control expenditures and to maximize cost-effectiveness. Bilingual directors should expect to be confronted with one financial crisis after another, particularly during the first few years of the program.

Suggested Activities

☐ *Maximize availability of resources.* Administrators should use the various staff members in a school system as resources. The local reading specialist can train bilingual language-arts specialists in areas relevant to bilingual education. School psychologists can conduct workshops for bilingual staff members if local counselors are not able to provide affective services. In addition, project administrators should seek additional revenues for materials at both local and state levels. By comparing the dollar value of resources to the actual cost of the bilingual program, evaluators can determine the level of fiscal effectiveness.

☐ *Share responsibility for expenditures.* While the director is meeting with teachers and administrators, resolving instructional issues, and developing a parent advisory council, another staff member (curriculum coordinator, secretary, administrative assistant, etc.) can be responsible for monitoring expenses. In this way, the program has a regularly scheduled summary of available monies and a procedure for expending resources when the director is absent. Most importantly, the director is free to devote more time to students and to instructional activities.

☐ *Allocate resources to needs effectively.* Quite often, new bilingual-education programs allocate too many of their resources to only one grade level or component (e.g., curriculum development). Evaluators should carefully consider each component's essential needs and distribute resources accordingly.

☐ *Establish qualifications for personnel.* In most programs, the single greatest expenditure is for staff salaries. Thus, it is vital that staff members fully meet the program's operational needs. If the project administrator has convinced the local school system of the value of bilingual education, the system will support the establishment of specific qualifications for bilingual personnel. Procedures may include language testing or requiring certain courses related to bilingual education. The evaluator reviews the existence of or lack of such special prerequisites in order to assess this activity.

·☐ *Establish personnel procedures.* The evaluator should assess the bilingual program's personnel specifications and the degree to which they conform to the local school system's personnel requirements. The personnel policies of the entire district must be reviewed to ensure that bilingual-program staff members receive the same treatment as other district personnel. Such policies as tenure should also be examined to ensure fairness. In this activity, the administrator must elicit the cooperation and support of key administrators in the school system.

☐ *Establish materials specifications.* Unfortunately, inappropriate materials are often purchased and used. During the early years of a program, a school system and its bilingual staff should continually review materials and local educational needs in order to identify purchasing specifications. Many monolingual school programs are beginning to recommend reading series, subject texts, and other kinds of materials for purchase throughout their districts. If a material is not on the approved list, a special request and review must be made before the material is purchased. In many instances, bilingual programs are developing similar lists to ensure that their limited materials funds are well spent and to involve teachers in an ongoing review of materials. In order to assess this process, the evaluator should examine the curriculum-development component to determine the efficacy of current procedures.

☐ *Establish procedures for controlling materials expenditures.* Unfortunately, too many programs set up annual purchase plans with the same percentages of funds being used in the same areas each year. For example, a bilingual program may set aside 10 percent of their curriculum dollars for math, 20 percent for reading, and so on. These percentages should not be fixed; rather they should be based on specifically identified needs. Teacher involvement is essential in the annual needs assessment. The program evaluator should examine purchasing patterns semiannually in order to ensure the existence of annual purchase priorities.

Monitoring and Coordinating Component Activities

Since a bilingual-education director oversees instruction, curriculum, staff training, and parent activities, the third management function is to monitor and coordinate component activities. In most educational programs, certain administrators are responsible for educational continuity. For example, supervisors of elementary education must ensure a vertical relationship between first-grade primer activities and second- and third-grade developmental reading activities. The local director of pupil personnel coordinates vocational counseling, career education, and psychological services. In a bilingual-education program, these two coordination requirements, as well as dozens of others, are the responsibility of the program administrator. Consequently, the director must be fully aware of local referral and implementation processes and must be willing to accept management and coordination responsibilities faced by few other school system administrators.

Suggested Activities

☐ *Ensure that planned activities contribute to overall program goals.* Pilot or experimental programs usually develop end-of-year goals, but project management should not wait until that time to determine which goals are being met and which activities have contributed to goal achievement. All component activities should be monitored continually, so that midyear changes can be made if certain processes are proving ineffective. Project management should examine staff-training activities and the degree to which training results in instructional changes. Community awareness should also be reviewed throughout the year. The evaluator's job is to determine how responsive management is to process assessments. A checklist of evaluatory recommendations and related management decisions can be developed.

☐ *Discover and resolve unforeseen problems.* In new educational programs, crisis situations often reach a peak before project administrators take action. The evaluator and the administrator can work together to improve crisis management by developing procedures that identify critical situations in their earliest stages. If the evaluation team provides semimonthly process reports, the director should be adequately informed of impending critical situations.

☐ *Ensure that individual components are compatible with and reinforce each other.* If certain participating schools or grade levels do not conform to the local program's operational model, the students will suffer. It is the project administrator's responsibility to see that all teachers and components are compatible with the local bilingual model. For example, a program should not use one approach to developmental reading at one grade level and another approach at a different grade level. Youngsters at one school cannot make the transition from Spanish to English reading at one level of proficiency while another participating school in the same district uses a different level of proficiency. The project director, through communications and meetings, must ensure standardization and mutually compatible processes. The evaluator examines the steps taken by the project director toward this end.

Working with Other Administrators

The final management function is to establish working relationships with other administrators. If bilingual education is to be successful in a school system, it must have the support of local administrators, particularly the principals of participating schools. The program director should continually interact with other administrators in the district, so that bilingual education will be viewed as an integral part of the local school system.

Suggested Activities

☐ *Involve participating schools in a needs assessment.* The federal government is continually taking steps to decentralize federal programming in schools. The rationale is twofold: to make education more relevant and to give educators an opportunity to influence educational plans on a local level. Bilingual-education administrators should participate in this decentralization process by conducting needs assessments on a building-by-building basis. Evaluators can assist the director in these efforts by reviewing language-test data and discussing the impact of the various tests, levels, and performances on program needs and designs. The evaluator can also design needs-assessment surveys, review the needs of incoming students, and summarize each year's growth rates on a school-by-school basis. Equipped with this data, the director can then meet with each building principal to review each building's needs in the area of bilingual education.

☐ *Coordinate planning efforts of participating schools.* The director should permit teachers and administrators to select and order materials for their own classes. At the same time, however, he or she should also eliminate any unnecessary duplication of spending. For example, if one building wants to purchase certain materials that will not be used on a daily basis, the director can consult with teachers and principals in other buildings to see if they are interested in sharing the materials. Furthermore, learning activities should be planned and coordinated so that a child moving from one building to another in the same school district will not suffer. The evaluator can determine if the program is following similar paths in different schools by making direct observations and by reviewing instructional topic plans.

☐ *Provide an orientation program for new teachers.* This activity is especially important, because it encourages coordinated communications and planning among participating schools. Each year the project director should plan two types of orientation, one for new teachers and one for all teachers. The evaluation should measure the impact of these preservice sessions on program effectiveness and interschool cooperation.

All of these management activities should be evaluated during a program's first year of implementation. Unfortunately, evaluators sometimes delay this process until they have reviewed a program's products, only to find that classroom difficulties frequently arise at the management level.

12 Parent Involvement in Evaluation

Most bilingual-program guidelines call for parent involvement in program activities — a marriage of requirement to need. The federal government requires parent involvement in federally funded bilingual education, and states are beginning to require similar levels of involvement. This chapter reviews specific parent-involvement activities related to evaluation.

For purposes of this discussion, the terms *community involvement* and *parent involvement* are synonymous. If one wishes to have a meaningful form of community involvement, especially in bilingual education, the community should certainly include parents of youngsters in the program.

Parent involvement in evaluation can take several forms, all of which should be written into the evaluation goals. Involvement is sequential — in other words, a group of parents masters certain evaluation skills or activities before moving on to the next level of involvement. The success of parent-involvement activities in evaluation is partially dependent on the degree to which the activities are acceptable to teachers, aides, and administrators. If they are introduced one at a time, the parent activities will be accepted more readily.

Parents as Advisors

At the first level of involvement, parents act as advisors. The evaluation team meets with the Parent Advisory Council (PAC) at the beginning of the academic year or before school starts. At that time, the evaluators ask the PAC to respond to the following questions:

☐ What are you, as parents, most concerned about regarding the bilingual education program?

☐ How do you feel about the current evaluation plans?

☐ Imagine that it is the end of the school year. What questions would you like to ask us about the program's activities during this school year?

☐ What are your priorities for the program and for evaluation?

☐ What do you dislike about evaluators?

Each of these questions gives the evaluators an opportunity to establish a two-way supportive relationship with the PAC. Further, each question provides insight into the parents' priorities, needs, and expectations. The meeting also gives the PAC information about evaluation activities before these activities are initiated and establishes open communications between the PAC and the evaluation team.

This level of involvement can continue throughout the academic year, with the evaluation team and the PAC meeting periodically. The meetings may take place just before and after the delivery of each evaluation report, or the PAC can create an evaluation subcommittee to meet with the evaluators on a more regular basis.

The PAC Evaluation Subcommittee

A PAC evaluation subcommittee can be used to bring local parents to the next level of involvement. At this step, parents move beyond the role of advisors and into the realm of data collection. Specifically, parents can be trained to interview other parents by telephone or at home. These parent-parent interviews are useful in measuring parent attitude toward:

☐ Bilingual education in general

☐ The local bilingual-education program

☐ Education and the value of schooling

☐ Certain program activities

Ideas for additional measurements can be generated by the PAC evaluation subcommittee. Frequently, subcommittees suggest ideas that significantly expand the scope of evaluation and provide greater services to the program and the PAC.

The evaluation subcommittee of the local PAC should be involved in developing the bilingual program's parent survey. Since parents usually do not have experience in item development, evaluation-team members should assist. Two approaches can be used. It may be most productive to provide the PAC evaluation subcommittee with previously used parent-interview questionnaires. In a mid-sized Massachusetts city, for example, the author provided the PAC subcommittee with four different parent surveys, each with its own unique format and questions. With these surveys in hand, each member of the subcommittee established priorities for questions and selected the most suitable format. The coordinator of the subcommittee then collected the data and identified the group's overall priority choices. The author used the second approach with a group of parents in New Bedford, Massachusetts. They were asked to list topics for inclusion in a parent survey. The author then developed survey items based on these PAC-generated topics and asked the PAC members to review the survey before it was printed.

Before training in actual interview techniques begins, PAC members should be advised that some of them may be asked to withdraw from participation as interviewers. Parents who are unable to separate themselves from personal issues during training and role playing, or who are unable to conduct discussions in each household's dominant language, should be eliminated from the interview team. Alternative tasks can be provided for them, such as tallying questionnaires, coordinating activities, and scheduling interviews.

Training consists of role playing and orientation exercises. Parents learn to conduct objective interviews, to avoid discussing personal situations (e.g., "My child's teacher said . . ."), and to understand and work toward the goals of the evaluation activity. Evaluators should be certain that participating PAC interviewers understand their relationship to the evaluation component and see themselves as extensions of the evaluation team.

After training, parent interviewers are ready to begin collecting data. The evaluation team randomly selects the parents of at least 10 percent of the bilingual children at each participating grade level to interview. The subcommittee members divide the interviews according to their own individual availabilities and neighborhoods. They telephone the selected interviewees for appointments if they are going to make home visits, or they complete the interviews by telephone. If the evaluation team does not wish to limit interviewees to those parents who have telephones, the interviewers can establish contact by mail and make arrangements for interviews at the school. The telephone approach is usually more responsive and certainly more expedient.

Parents who conduct interviews or help conduct the survey should be paid for their efforts. An equitable rate is the local hourly salary for beginning bilingual teacher aides.

Throughout the interviewing process, parents acquire skills and become involved in activities that enhance the overall impact of the PAC. Without a doubt, each of these evaluation subcommittees becomes significantly more aware of bilingual-education activities. In addition, they realize how PACs can assist school activities and how PAC activities can reach out to parents.

Parents as Testing Assistants

A third level of parent involvement is assisting in or actually administering certain tests. In Haverstraw, New York, the author trained several parents to administer the *John T. Dailey Language Facility Test* and the *Walker Readiness Test.* These instruments are bilingual and are administered on an individualized basis. Parents were thoroughly trained and were continually cautioned about test idiosyncrasies and student behaviors. These parents and others have demonstrated that highly specialized training in educational research is not necessary to administer certain tests properly. However, extensive training by professional evaluators is required.

The Haverstraw parents received three hours of training for each test. In any such training program, parents should learn the significance of each test question and how to respond to various kinds of answers. After role playing with each other, testing assistants practice with a nonprogram class.

There are many advantages and benefits when parents become involved in the collection of test data. First, evaluation teams are able to collect more individualized data within the same budgetary and time constraints. In addition, this nonthreatening involvement of parents is an appropriate way to introduce teachers to parent involvement in evaluation. Finally, the task itself is very meaningful for the parents, the bilingual PAC, and other community representatives.

Certain tests, such as the *John T. Dailey Language Facility Test*, require the test administrator to motivate the child to describe a photograph. The examiner then records every word of the child's description. The latter task requires that the parent assistant be able to take verbatim dictation fast enough so as not to interrupt the child's discussion. Such special administration skills must be verified before a parent is approved as a testing assistant.

If a parent is unable to remain totally objective while administering a test, he or she should not be allowed to continue testing. Some parents unconsciously provide too much help for children and actually "teach" the test. This tendency is easily observed and can usually be remedied.

All tests cannot be administered by parent evaluators. Many of the reading diagnostic tests are beyond the capability of parents who have not had formal education. Furthermore, some parents lack the language facility necessary to administer bilingual instruments. In this situation, the evaluation staff can establish teams and allow certain parents to administer tests only in their dominant languages.

In addition to administering individualized tests, parents can assist evaluators and teachers with group tests. For example, many evaluators ask parents to help with nearly all the *Inter-American* reading tests and with English standardized tests. Parents can distribute tests, explain directions to individual children who need assistance, review the student-written information at the top of each test, and proctor throughout the testing period. They can also be trained to check if children are turning pages and completing test sections.

Usually everyone concerned is happy when parents assist with testing. Parents are associated with professional evaluation activities and are being paid for their services. Teachers receive additional objective and individualized feedback on their students. Children benefit from individual attention, and evaluators can provide a more well-rounded evaluation model and data bank.

Parents as Classroom Observers

Some evaluation teams use parents to provide observation data about the classroom. If parents participate in this manner, they should be extensively trained and the relationship between parents and teachers must be strong. Teachers should first meet with the evaluation coordinator and the program director to review and modify the observation instruments the parent observers will use. The observation instruments should not qualitatively assess teachers. Rather, they should measure the degree to which bilingual education and locally developed process goals are implemented.

Parents can collect observation data in these areas:

- [ ] Existence of small-group or individualized instruction
- [ ] Amount of teacher-directed, as opposed to student-centered, activities
- [ ] Utilization of dominant-language instruction
- [ ] Utilization of bilingual materials
- [ ] Utilization of teacher aides for reinforcement activities
- [ ] Other quantitative assessment factors determined by teachers and parents

After the teachers, the program director, and the evaluator have reviewed the data-collection instruments, they should meet with the parent observers. The parents and teachers can then discuss each item, its relevance to bilingual education, and problems related to additional adults being in the classroom. The evaluator acts as a coordinator, working to sensitize each group to the other's needs. The meeting concludes with the two groups agreeing on a series of common goals.

If the parents and teachers participate in a series of values-clarification activities, they will grow personally and will be more willing to tear down some of the walls that exist between them. Most barriers between parents and teachers are built of irrational fears. Many parents fear that teachers regard them as uneducated and inferior; in turn, many teachers feel that their jobs are threatened by parent evaluation teams. This fear is more prevalent among non-Hispanic teachers who are part of a teaching team or who are fluent in Spanish but are not native speakers. There are several books on values clarification that contain activities appropriate for a diverse group of teachers and parents.

If the program wishes to involve parents in classroom evaluation activities but does not want them to collect specific data, parents may observe the classrooms in an unstructured fashion. Under such a plan, parents and teachers meet to discuss bilingual education and its relationship to classroom activities, the special needs of participating youngsters, dominant-language instruction, and other educational concepts and practices. After such a session, parents are scheduled to visit classrooms, where they are encouraged to jot down any notes they wish. Following this, the parents complete a questionnaire that asks the following open-ended questions:

- [ ] Briefly describe the observed activities.

- [ ] What were two things observed that you particularly liked?

- [ ] Was there anything that you disliked? If so, please describe it.

- [ ] If you could make any changes in the classroom you observed, what would those changes be?

This is a simple way to identify strengths and weaknesses as perceived by parents. Follow-up should be part of the process. Participating parents and teachers meet to discuss the parents' observations. Prior to this meeting, it is essential that evaluators review their observations in order to eliminate any inappropriate misinterpretations or information. For example, a parent might assess classroom activities that have little or nothing to do with the bilingual instructional model. In a similar evaluation activity, one parent was particularly concerned about playground distractions just outside the bilingual classroom. These activities were irrelevant to bilingual instruction as such. In this instance, the evaluator directed the parent to the building principal for discussion. Although the parent had a valid observation and made a reasonable criticism, such comments might jeopardize the previously established relationship between parent and teacher. The evaluator should also eliminate any comments that pertain solely to teacher personality or arise from personal biases.

If possible, it is a good idea to discuss these types of evaluation activities with the local teachers' organization or union before implementation. In this way, the bilingual-program evaluator can assure the organization that parents will be assessing degree of program implementation, not teacher performance or quality.

Contributing to the Evaluation Report

Parents can also contribute to the evaluator's report by providing written summaries of their evaluation activities and their observations. As with all other activities, training is important. In this instance, parents should be trained to:

- [ ] Identify strengths as well as weaknesses

- [ ] Remain objective

- [ ] Offer recommendations

- [ ] Discuss program activities rather than specific teaching behaviors

The evaluator may include a disclaimer in the introduction to the report. The disclaimer might read: "Opinions expressed by the parents do not necessarily reflect the opinions of the evaluation team." In this way, parent input is identified as supplemental data rather than as part of the evaluators' formal conclusions.

13 Evaluating Parent Involvement

The preceding chapter primarily discusses involving parents in actual program assessment. Participation in the evaluation component is a meaningful form of parent involvement. However, bilingual-education programs, in general, also involve parents in a variety of other activities, including:

☐ Workshops in which parents learn how to reinforce their children's education

☐ Classes that upgrade basic skills and provide ESL instruction

☐ Bicultural activities in which parents learn about each other's customs, foods, holidays, and so forth

☐ Newsletters that inform parents about school activities and provide helpful hints

☐ Program councils that advise the administration about decision-making, coordinate parent-teacher bilingual activities, and approve each year's program modifications

These and other activities are found in varying degrees in almost all bilingual-education projects. Some bilingual programs, such as those in the Chicago school system, have implemented unusually strong parent components. There are parent rooms in the various schools, full-time parent coordinators, and many parent training activities. Although larger cities are likely to have more funds and available staff, a number of smaller school systems are, for the first time, involving Hispanic parents in many different ways.

In order to conduct a broad-based evaluation, bilingual-education evaluators must assess program impact on parents. Although debates still rage on, there have been enough research findings to validate the hypothesis that parent involvement does affect a child's educational potential. Those programs that make a concerted effort to involve parents in educational activities show a marked difference from programs that do not. The author conducted one such study in Wethersfield, Connecticut. That school system experimented with an incentive program. The staff advised a certain number of parents about their children's learning goals and offered rewards to both parent and child if the learning goals were met. In other classes, children were advised of the learning goals, but the parents were not. Children whose parents received cards outlining the learning activities for each coming week showed criterion-referenced achievement rates that were higher than those demonstrated by youngsters in classes without parent involvement. At the present time, this project has not been replicated, but it does raise significant questions that program planners cannot afford to ignore.

When reviewing parent-involvement programs, the evaluator should ask:

☐ Are parents aware of the value of education?

☐ Do parents understand the need for bilingual instruction?

☐ Do parents understand their role in instilling values as part of education?

☐ Do parents understand how they can reinforce school instruction?

☐ Is the Parent Advisory Council carrying out the functions it established for itself?

The evaluator's role varies according to the parent-involvement activities implemented. For example, during a program's early years, general parent awareness is very often a high priority; however, parent-training workshops usually do not become a part of a program's model until after the first year. After several years of programming and modification, parent-involvement activities might be expanded, perhaps to include parents in evaluation. Thus, the evaluator's assessment activities must be adjusted annually, depending on parent-involvement priorities.

During a program's first few years, the evaluator should consider personally interviewing 10 percent of the participating parents. Interviewees are randomly selected, but should be stratified by serviced grade level, neighborhood, ethnic group, and any other demographic breakdown that would lend more substance to the analysis. In most instances, it is impossible for the evaluation team to conduct all the personal interviews. This is an opportunity to get PAC members involved in evaluation activities. These interviews rarely take place during the opening months of a program's first year. Due to many critical problems confronting project administrators, staff members, and evaluators on a day-to-day basis, a parent survey usually is a low priority. Consequently, personal interviews should be postponed until late spring. They can then provide data for evaluating the program's first year and can serve as baseline data for a pre-post second-year measurement.

After 10 percent of the target parents have been personally interviewed, the remaining 90 percent can be given a take-home survey. Take-home surveys are not distributed until all personal interviews are completed, since the evaluator usually must draw on nonselected parents to complete the interview group. A small percentage of parents will not wish to participate in the interview for personal reasons, and some parents will not be at the telephone number and address provided by the schools.

Surveying Parents

The Parent Attitude Survey (Appendix H) can be used as a take-home instrument at various stages of a program's development. Some items relate to parent awareness of bilingual-education programming. Others deal with parent attitudes toward education in general and bilingual education in particular. Parent surveys should always be available in all community languages.

Interview data and take-home data are analyzed separately. It is important that all parent-awareness data be analyzed across items rather than with total scores. The evaluator must address each item individually; of course, certain items can subsequently be grouped to reveal trends or lack of trends. In a narrative report, the evaluator need only discuss those items that are relevant at the time. Items that are not in need of staff or administrative attention can be summarized together. On a pre-post basis, evaluators may discuss growth or change if they use descriptive statistics rather than inferential statistics (for example, percentages rather than t-scores).

Social Indicators

In addition to collecting data with the Parent Attitude Survey, the evaluator of a bilingual program can use social indicators to measure program effectiveness. For example, if a program hopes to increase the amount of parent involvement in homework activities, teachers can, from time to time, advise their students that a parent signature or check mark is required on classroom worksheets or homework papers. If the program conducts workshops with specifically stated goals, the evaluator can use social indicators to measure the achievement of those goals. For example, if the aim of a particular workshop is to get parents involved in education activities at home, the evaluator might look at social indicators such as:

- ☐ How many parents bring their children to get library cards?
- ☐ How many parents know when educational television shows are being broadcast?
- ☐ How many parents attend an ESL or GED program?

The use of social indicators requires a certain amount of flexibility on the part of all concerned. Each indicator cited can be criticized in one way or another. Is the library close enough to the Hispanic neighborhood? Is educational programming aired at reasonable hours? The Parent Advisory Council, bilingual teachers, and other stakeholders can be helpful in choosing appropriate social indicators to assess the bilingual program's impact on parent attitudes.

Questionnaires, especially if they are validated with personal interviews, and relevant social indicators provide a program with a better understanding of parent awareness than do more traditional models that rely on student attendance, parent attendance at meetings, and other culturally biased benchmarks. The results of such evaluation should have a direct impact on management's approach to parent involvement. If the evaluator presents a comprehensive analysis of data, the project administrator should be able to identify successful dissemination mechanisms, appropriate parent workshops, and positive PAC experiences.

14 Evaluation Conclusions and Recommendations

A comprehensive evaluation directly affects teacher-training activities, curriculum development, instructional scheduling, and program design. The program strengths and weaknesses revealed help administrators establish priorities for the next year. If an evaluation component continually expands into new program areas on an annual basis, certain areas must eventually be excluded for lack of time and resources. By the same token, if one area shows a particular strength for two consecutive years, evaluation activities related to that area can be eliminated and replaced with investigation into identified areas of program weakness.

Identifying Program Weaknesses

To guide the less experienced evaluator, this chapter presents a series of program shortcomings that seem to be widespread. The author observed each described weakness in a least 20 different situations. They include:

☐ *Lack of remedial reading in Spanish.* Most schools offer English remedial reading for English-dominant children who are two or more years behind in reading. The same kinds of processes should be offered in Spanish to Spanish-dominant or transitional readers who are far below the norm.

☐ *Lack of parallel ESL/bilingual instruction at the readiness level.* At the kindergarten and first-grade levels, Spanish-dominant children should be developing their reading skills in Spanish. At the same time, their ESL activities should introduce English oral language *and* reinforce whatever readiness activities have already taken place in Spanish. For example, if shapes and colors are being reviewed in Spanish reading readiness, the kindergarten ESL lesson could cover the same ground.

☐ *Inappropriate use of bilingual teacher aides.* If a bilingual program uses English-dominant teachers assisted by bilingual paraprofessionals, the evaluator should determine the degree to which the paraprofessional provides initial instruction. Each child should receive initial instruction from a certified teacher in the child's dominant language.

☐ *Lack of comprehensive academic subjects in Spanish.* All too often, a bilingual teacher working with Spanish-dominant children teaches only reading or language arts. Spanish-dominant children should receive most of their academic program (math, science, social studies, etc.) in Spanish, with English-language instruction increasing as their English skills improve. The evaluator should review schedules, plans, and actual lesson presentations in order to identify reasons for academic growth or lack of growth in Spanish.

☐ *Lack of similarity between English reading and Spanish reading curriculum materials.* Children should not change text modality or approach to developmental reading when they make the transition into second-language reading. Basal series, workbooks, and linguistic approaches should be reviewed by teachers and evaluators in order to ensure that children do not have to relearn skills before they make the transition.

If data collection and analysis are to provide useful conclusions and recommendations, these are the kinds of topics evaluators must address. If an evaluator merely states that "50 percent of the children achieved the anticipated growth rates" without discussing the implications of this statistic, the program has not received a true evaluation. The collection, analysis, and presentation of data related to growth rates should be accompanied by recommendations regarding all program components and processes. Again, the evaluator must take care not to stray outside the realm of evaluation into a supervisory role. Teacher capabilities, teacher personalities, or individual training needs should not be discussed.

Reporting Mechanisms

In addition to understanding the political, sociological, and educational ramifications of evaluation recommendations, an evaluator should use various reporting mechanisms, including:

- ☐ Evaluation design report
- ☐ Implementation/interim evaluation reports
- ☐ Monthly communications memos
- ☐ Parent feedback sessions
- ☐ Staff orientation and feedback sessions
- ☐ Final evaluation report

The evaluation design report, or the evaluation package, highlights and explains the evaluation design and the processes to be implemented. It should be presented to program administrators and teachers in workshop sessions early in the year. After giving the participants a "guided tour" of the evaluation format, the evaluator reviews each objective and the plan for measuring achievement of the objective. This session can also be used to give staff members an opportunity to contribute to the evaluation design by commenting on performance levels, program expectations, and other design facets (see Chapter 3). This report and the accompanying orientation sessions give teachers and administrators a sense of authorship in the evaluation plan: a group of outsiders is not coming in to assess program effectiveness. The so-called outside group thus establishes a strong link with staff members prior to plan implementation.

The second major report, the implementation/interim report, is used to review program processes and the degree to which each activity is contributing to the achievement of program goals. If this report is presented in February of the academic year, sufficient time has elapsed to assess activities, yet there is still time to initiate midstream changes if called for.

Monthly Evaluation Memo

Evaluation Tasks Implemented	Evaluation Problems Encountered	Observations/Findings	Related Plans for Future Evaluations
1. Individualized readiness testing	1. Two teachers were not aware of testing schedule.	1. Many children were unable to take the test in Spanish.	1. Other group tests to be given by teachers
2. Meeting with program teachers	2. None	2. All teachers seem cooperative and supportive of evaluation activities.	2. Will meet with teachers after prescores are analyzed
3. Meeting with principals	3. One principal was upset because he did not receive last year's report.	3. Communication between bilingual office and principals needs to be increased.	3. Will give principals a confidential survey in April
4. Comparison-group testing	4. One teacher in the control group is using bilingual methods.	4. All tests administered.	4. Considering eliminating bilingual teacher from comparisons

This report can also summarize results of parent surveys, non-program staff surveys, teacher self-evaluation surveys, and teacher-aide surveys. Modifications to the instructional system and staff training plans can be based on this report.

Prior to the submission of a final evaluation report, other communication mechanisms can be implemented. At the beginning of the academic year, the evaluator should meet with the Parent Advisory Council to introduce and explain the entire evaluation plan and the role of the evaluator. Furthermore, during this first meeting with parents, a parent subcommittee on evaluation may be formed to work with the evaluation team throughout the academic year (see Chapter 12). Communications with the parent council at large take place in two additional workshop sessions, one following the interim report and the other after the final report. Similar sessions can be held with all the program's staff members. Evaluatory findings are presented to teachers and administrators in group sessions and to each individual staff member shortly after on-site observations.

These meetings reinforce and update the monthly memos from the evaluation team to the project administration. These memos, like the one on page 91, communicate important evaluation observations that should not have to wait until the next major report is due. This monthly form, brief as it is, makes the overall evaluation more meaningful and timely.

The final evaluation report summarizes and unifies all previous communications on student growth. In other words, if the interim evaluation report discussed the results of the Bilingual Teacher Self-Evaluation Scale (Appendix E) and various teaching skills, the final evaluation report, most of which deals with student growth and group growth rates, should somehow relate the interim comments to the growth rates. For example, if teachers perceived themselves as weak in certain bilingual teaching skills, did that weakness manifest itself in a lack of growth in the corresponding areas?

The final evaluation report reviews student progress in the subject areas by grade level. Spanish reading, English reading, mathematics, and each of the other measured content areas are discussed. In order to keep individual teachers anonymous, schools and classrooms are never identified.

15 Utilizing the Evaluation Review Instrument

The Evaluation Review Instrument (Appendix J), based on an instrument initially developed by HEW, reviews the evaluation design. If a bilingual-program evaluator is inexperienced or if there is no official program evaluator, the ERI can guide the development of an evaluation plan by assisting staff members in planning measurably stated process and product objectives, comparability, baseline data, and noninstructional evaluation activities.

In order for the ERI to be an effective tool, staff members must want their program to rate highly on the instrument. This desire can be internally or externally motivated. Using the ERI, colleagues or program administrators review the proposed design and report their findings to the evaluator before evaluation implementation. If this process is too threatening, the evaluator can hire an evaluation auditor. Auditing of evaluation designs is required by some states for certain programs. For example, in the state of Massachusetts, if a Title I program evaluates itself and does not work with an outside evaluator, it must contract with an outside auditor. The auditor uses the ERI or another form to assess the evaluation design and the implementation of evaluation activities. External auditors can be helpful even if their services are not required by state regulations. The HEW Title VII office conducted several educational audit conferences during the early seventies. Each of these conferences produced a list of certified auditors trained to comprehensively audit evaluation plans and evaluation activities.

Part I of the instrument examines the evaluation design; Part II assesses actual evaluation activities. This latter section documents the evaluation team's efficiency, scheduling practices, and ability to coordinate their own activities. Part III of the ERI reviews the evaluation team's recommendations. Frequently, appropriately scheduled and implemented evaluation models lead to irrelevant and inappropriate recommendations. If this happens on a local level, the last section of the ERI will document discrepancies and signal a need for change.

16 Bilingual-Program Evaluation: A National Survey

Prior to the development of this book, the author conducted a survey of 400 bilingual-education programs throughout the country. This chapter is a review of the data generated by that survey. In a sense, it is a personal interview with many bilingual educators. All the questions were related to evaluation techniques and instruments. Interest was very high, with 72 bilingual administrators responding. This high return rate to an unsolicited questionnaire speaks well for the future of bilingual education and demonstrates the amount of current interest in objective measurement. All comments cited were repeated at least three times.

Reading Readiness and Early Childhood

The first question on the survey asked administrators to list all Spanish-language reading readiness or early-childhood developmental tests used to evaluate their bilingual-education activities. They were also asked to express their opinions about the tests. Here is a sampling of their comments:

☐ Tests are more useful if they measure readiness and language dominance. The *Pictorial Test of Bilingualism and Language Dominance* does this very well.

☐ The *James Language Dominance Test* is especially useful at kindergarten and early primary levels and is quite easy to administer, making it suitable for paraprofessional use.

☐ The *Inter-American Series* is very easy to administer but does not require any talking or language production by the child.

☐ The *Tests of Basic Experiences (TOBE)* are good readiness measurements, but include a few items that are culturally confusing to Hispanics.

☐ The *Metropolitan Readiness Tests* are available only in English. A local Spanish version was approved by the publisher.

☐ The *Peabody Picture Vocabulary Test* does not have an officially published Spanish version available. Local editions seem to be effective.

☐ The *Boehm Test of Basic Concepts* is good, but needs to have Spanish manuals and supplementary materials developed.

☐ The *BABEL Language Test* is not totally effective, but seems to work well if a program is using the *BABEL* readiness materials.

☐ The *SOBER* approaches are good, but assume that one is using the phonetic approach to instruction in later reading development.

Reading and Writing

The second question on the survey asked administrators to list any Spanish-language reading or writing tests used in their elementary bilingual-education programs and to comment about each.

☐ The *SOBER* test is effective with the SRA objectives and has an excellent management system.

☐ The *Santillana Program Management System* has been effective. It is geared toward specific mastery level tests; sometimes it is clumsy to use, but it has been good for evaluation purposes.

☐ The *Inter-American* series has been helpful in measuring

growth, but is not geared toward any specific objectives.

☐ The Spanish *ROLL* criterion-referenced tests are excellent if one is using the *ROLL* reading program (self-paced, immediate feedback, etc.).

☐ Locally developed Spanish-comprehension assessment instruments based on the Laidlaw series (*Por el mundo del cuento y la aventura*) are used often.

☐ The *Input Test of Spanish Comprehension* has an interesting approach; it uses a modified close procedure.

☐ The Los Angeles Developmental Reading Program has Spanish criterion-referenced tests that are useful.

☐ The Puerto Rican Spanish reading tests are like the *Inter-American* tests and seem to be appropriate in most instances, but they do not provide appropriate normative data. The Puerto Rican tests have certain advantages over the *Inter-American* batteries: fewer items per page, larger pictures, and fewer words that are unicultural.

Oral Language

The third survey question asked bilingual-program administrators to identify useful oral-language tests. They responded as follows:

☐ The *Bilingual Syntax Measure* (*BSM*) is very helpful. Unfortunately, it is limited since it does not measure vocabulary acquisition.

☐ The *Linguistic Capacity Index* is very useful.

☐ The *James Language Dominance Test* is used to measure oral language at the elementary level.

☐ The *Basic Inventory of Natural Language* (*BINL*) measures oral language. It has variable and prescriptive applications, but is quite time-consuming.

☐ Moreno's *Oral English Proficiency Placement Test* and *Oral Spanish Proficiency Placement Test* are successful instruments, especially at the kindergarten level.

☐ *Dos Amigos* is a vocabulary-based instrument used at preschool and early primary levels. It is easy to administer and appropriate for identifying language dominance.

Oral-language instruments have significantly increased in number during the last few years. Literally dozens of locally developed instruments were also named by respondents. However, most of these instruments are being used in conjunction with one of the commercially available instruments. The three tests most often named were the *James Language Dominance Test*, the *Bilingual Syntax Measure*, and the *Basic Inventory of Natural Language (BINL)*.

Science and Social Studies

Bilingual educators were also asked to list elementary science and social studies tests in Spanish: not one of the respondents could name any tests that are presently commercially available. At this time, there are very few resources in this area. The Puerto Rican Department of Instruction has tests in particular disciplines available. However, their science and social studies instruments are geared for local curriculum guides. The same can be said about the elementary-level tests developed by the Mexico City Office of Education. The Bilingual Education Applied Research Unit (BEARU) of Hunter College in New York City has developed an extensive series of elementary science objectives. The objectives, expressed in behavioral terms, could easily dictate or define test items. Lack of tests in science and social studies is not unique to bilingual education. Monolingual English elementary education is not replete with standardized instruments in these areas either. For now, bilingual programs should use their curriculum guides or the suggested objectives from Hunter College to develop their own instruments.

Affective Domain

In addition to asking about cognitive instrumentation, the survey also asked about affective yardsticks. Response was limited due to lack of available instruments.

☐ Teaching Resources has several Spanish self-concept and attitude scales. However, pretest scores on the *Primary Self-Concept Inventory* are usually too high for the students to achieve further growth. Self-concept tests should be delayed until the eighth or ninth week of the academic year. Early administration often results in very high self-concept scores, scores that are both unrealistic and unrelated to the educational process.

Evaluation Problems

One of the more interesting questions on the survey asked

bilingual educators to identify their "greatest problem in developing and implementing an evaluation." Responses were wide ranging. Suggestions for dealing with the problem follow each response.

☐ *Articulating objectives that staff members can "buy into," stating procedures relating to each objective, and involving staff in data-collection activities.* The active participation of staff is essential to the eventual success of an evaluation. Using the format for developing objectives and related evaluation procedures (Chapter 3), the program evaluator should conduct a preservice or in-service session with all staff members. At that session, staff members are trained to develop objectives. After being divided by grade level or discipline area, they develop objectives prior to leaving the session. In this way, they feel a sense of authorship and perhaps become more interested in the overall evaluation component.

☐ *Lack of statistical analysis among all proficiency tests.* The "purists" among bilingual-program evaluators must adjust their standards if they are to measure oral-language abilities or proficiences. None of the oral-language tests have been normed to the extent required for inferential statistics. One must, therefore, rely on criterion-referenced performance levels or other kinds of descriptive analyses. The traditional approach to statistical analysis cannot be applied to most of the currently available oral-language measuring devices, and nothing can be done to the scoring systems to make them statistically legitimate.

☐ *Lack of comparison or control groups.* Many respondents indicated that teachers are fearful of bilingual-program evaluations. They do not wish to cooperate because they feel that the evaluator wants the comparison group to fail or, at least, to score lower than the program group. Several steps can be taken to encourage greater participation among comparison-group teachers. First, they can review data-analysis procedures and receive assurances that classrooms, teachers, and students will not be identified. Students can be assigned identification numbers to assure anonymity. If need be, an evaluator can combine all comparison teachers at a given grade level, eliminating any possible identification. Furthermore, if evaluators explain the "gap-reduction" approach to evaluation, pointing out that the intent is to reduce the gap between the program and the comparison groups, teachers may be more willing to comply. When they understand the gap-reduction approach, they no longer fear the traditional approach, which calls for the experimental students to outperform the comparison students.

☐ *Lack of standardized tests in Spanish.* Unfortunately, even if standardized tests were available in Spanish, there would probably be major differences between the Chicano groups of the Southwest, the Puerto Rican groups of the Northeast, and the Cuban groups of the Southeast. National Hispanic norms would be ruled invalid. Local norms are not difficult to develop, and regional norms can be developed on a cooperative basis. If a regional organization or a statewide group of bilingual programs works with a university or a statistical consultant, they can establish the local norms required to measure growth in statistical fashion.

These problems, of course, are just some of the more salient difficulties confronting evaluators of bilingual-education programs. Programs today lack historical data and experienced bilingual-evaluation teams. Because bilingual education is still an emerging process, evaluation of program components is a continually evolving concept as well. As bilingual programs mature and become increasingly effective, bilingual administrators and educators can expect to see similar advances in the area of assessment procedures, instruments, and personnel.

Appendix A

Individual Gain Rates

Name	Pretest grade equivalency	Previous average gain rate	Anticipated posttest grade equivalency	Actual posttest grade	✓

Appendix B

Performance Objective Outline

Product Objective #1	
Target population	A
Desired behavior	B
Performance level	C
Operational condition	D
Instrument	E

Evaluation Plan	
General technique	
Baseline data	
Sample group(s)	
Collection dates	
Data analysis	

Appendix C

Teacher-Interview Questionnaire

I. Student Background

1. How are students selected for the program?
2. How are students defined as Spanish dominant or English dominant?
3. How well do the students read in their dominant languages at this grade level?

II. Classroom Structure

4. Is your classroom an open classroom? Self-contained? Any other specific model? Is the model applicable to bilingual teaching?
5. Is there a team-teaching design? If so, does it function within or across grade levels? Is this method applicable to bilingual teaching?
6. How would you change or modify the structure of your classroom (scheduling, grouping, etc.)?
7. How many students are in your class?
8. How many Spanish-dominant students are in the class?
9. How many English-dominant students are in the class?
10. Are you bilingual?
11. Is there an aide? Is he or she bilingual?
12. Are there materials available for the students to use by themselves?

III. Spanish-Language Instruction to Spanish-Dominant Students

13. What kinds of Spanish-language instruction do Spanish-dominant students receive (group or individual)?
14. Which subjects are taught in Spanish to Spanish-dominant students?
15. Which subjects are taught in English and then reinforced in Spanish?
16. How much time is spent on Spanish instruction?
17. Who does most of this Spanish instruction?
18. What basic Spanish-language materials are available in each subject? Are there enough basic materials? Is their quality acceptable?
19. What supplementary materials are used? Are there enough supplementary materials? Is their quality acceptable?

20. What other materials would you like to include?
21. Are there any materials that you feel are inappropriate?

IV. Spanish-Language Instruction to English-Dominant Students

22. What kinds of SSL instruction do English-dominant students receive (group or individual)?
23. Which subjects are taught in Spanish to English-dominant students?
24. How much time is spent on Spanish instruction for English-dominant students?
25. Who teaches the SSL instruction?
26. What basic materials are available for SSL? Are there enough basic materials? Is their quality acceptable?
27. What other materials would you like to include?
28. What supplementary materials are available? Are there enough supplementary materials? Is their quality acceptable?
29. Are there any materials you consider inappropriate?

V. English-as-a-Second-Language and English Reading for Spanish-Dominant Students

30. What kind of instruction in ESL and English reading is given (group or individual)?
31. How much time is spent on ESL and English reading for Spanish-dominant students?
32. Who teaches ESL and English reading to Spanish-dominant students?
33. What basic materials are used? Are there enough basic materials? Is their quality acceptable?
34. What supplementary materials are available? Are there enough supplementary materials? Is their quality acceptable?
35. What other materials would you like to include?
36. Is there a relationship between oral ESL and English-reading lessons?
37. When do Spanish-dominant students begin to receive reading instruction in English?
38. How is the reading transition to English made? When does it begin?

VI. Paraprofessionals

39. How much time per day does the aide spend in the classroom?
40. What are the specific duties of the aide?

VII. Parent Involvement

41. Are parents encouraged to visit the classroom freely?
42. Describe any formal parent-visitation program or parent-awareness program.

VIII. Communications

43. Is the project director readily available when needed?
44. Do you receive communications about meetings, workshops, etc.?
45. Is project administration sensitive to classroom needs?
46. What kind of relationship exists between bilingual-program personnel and other administrators and teachers in the school district?

Appendix D

Sociogram Response Sheet

	Practice	Practice
Play	A	E
Work	B	F
Sit	C	G
Lead	D	

Appendix E

Bilingual-Teacher Self-Evaluation Scale

Directions: Please respond to each of the following items. This is an anonymous survey and will only be used to develop in-service training priorities and consultations. Check one answer for each statement.

1. My language skills can be identified as:

   Monolingual English _____

   Monolingual Spanish _____

   Transitional with English strength _____

   Transitional with Spanish strength _____

   Bilingual _____

   Don't know _____

2. In my classroom, Spanish-dominant children receive initial-reading instruction in Spanish.

   Yes _____

   No _____

3. In my classroom, concepts introduced in Spanish are reinforced in English:

   Daily _____

   Weekly _____

   Rarely _____

   Never _____

   Don't know _____

4. In my classroom, concepts introduced in English are reinforced in Spanish:

   Daily _____

   Weekly _____

   Rarely _____

   Never _____

   Don't know _____

	I am adequately trained in this area.	I have received no training in this area.	I have received some training in this area, but feel I need more.
5. Providing receptive and productive language development			
6. Developing auditory and visual discrimination skills			
7. Developing listening skills (sequences, recalls, etc.)			
8. Interrelating language development and concept development			
9. Encouraging open-ended, creative use of language			
10. Identifying language dominance			
11. Identifying specific reading problems			
12. Developing lessons based on contrastive analysis			
13. Modeling Spanish			
14. Modeling English			
15. Using activities other than printed exercises to develop syntactically accurate language			
16. Using counseling techniques and behavior modification to manage deviant behavior			
17. Helping students build self-discipline (contracting, continuous progress, etc.)			
18. Presenting language lessons sequentially to prevent pupil frustration			

Appendix F

Identification of Bilingual-Paraprofessional Training Needs

Plans are being made for in-service training of teacher aides. You, the teachers, can greatly assist us by answering the following questions. This is an anonymous survey and will be used only to design training sessions for the aides.

1. Listed below are six general tasks that may be the responsibility of the teacher aides on a regular basis. Please rank order in the spaces below the three training areas that would most benefit your aide. Also rank order three areas in which the aide is already proficient.

   A. Provides individual reading assistance to remedial-level students

   B. Relates to individual students and the group as a whole

   C. Performs clerical tasks competently (takes attendance, corrects tests, etc.)

   D. Provides emotional support to problem students (uses appropriate techniques)

   E. Tutors in areas other than reading, specifically ESL and oral-language development

   F. Reinforces math lessons in Spanish or English when class is divided into groups

	Areas of Proficiency	*Areas That Should Be Included in a Training Program*
1.	_____	_____
2.	_____	_____
3.	_____	_____

   Comments:

2. Aides should be able to upgrade the children's language skills. From the topics listed below, rank order those areas that should be included in a training program. Also rank order your aide's areas of proficiency.

   A. Understands linguistic structures and analyzes errors (linguistic interferences, tenses, etc.)

   B. Uses idiomatic expressions and vocabulary in both languages

   C. Applies remedial-reading and ESL techniques (use of context, oral-aural, etc.)

   D. Reinforces writing skills

   E. Uses special equipment (tape recorders, Language Master, etc.)

	Areas That Should Be Included
Areas of Proficiency	*in a Training Program*
1. _____	1. _____
2. _____	2. _____
3. _____	3. _____

   Comments:

3. The aide should be able to establish rapport with the class, behave in a professional manner, and give the student an adult ear if you are not available. From the topics listed below, rank order those areas that should be included in a training program. Also rank order your aide's areas of proficiency.

   A. Understands aspects of child development that enable him/her to cope with student behavior and problems

   B. Understands the specific problems of the local target population

C. Demonstrates a sense of compassion for the children and still keeps a professional distance

D. Encourages students to become an integral part of the class

Areas of Proficiency	*Areas That Should Be Included in a Training Program*
1. _____	1. _____
2. _____	2. _____
3. _____	3. _____

Comments:

Appendix G

Curriculum Review

Please select one series or individual item that you use to teach ESL, SSL, or Spanish reading. Answer the following questions about the material you have chosen.

1. Name of series or item:

2. For which language group (Spanish dominant, English dominant, bilingual) is this material most appropriate? With what size of group is this material best used?

3. How would you rate the material's appeal to children (colors, characters, etc.)?

4. Are exercises sequentially arranged according to your teaching needs?

5. Are there enough reinforcement exercises?

6. Can the students understand and follow the instructions without constant support from teachers?

7. Assess the physical manageability of this material (storage, ease of handling, etc.).

8. Is the material durable?

9. Is the cost of the material appropriate to its use in the classroom?

10. How does this material relate to other materials on the same level? In other words, does it have a good horizontal relationship?

11. How does it relate to materials used before and after it as far as difficulty is concerned? In other words, does it have a vertical relationship with other materials?

12. Does this material require extensive preparation on the part of the teacher?

13. Can this material be used by a paraprofessional or instructional aide? If so, must the teacher supervise the aide while the material is being used?

Appendix H

Parent Attitude Survey: English Version

Teacher should check one box identifying the language skills of the child whose parents are completing the questionnaire.

Spanish dominant ☐

English dominant ☐

Bilingual ☐

Directions. Please answer each question. If you do not have an answer, check "don't know." This is an anonymous questionnaire; you do not have to put your name on this paper.

1. Is your child involved in a bilingual-education classroom?

   Yes _____ No _____ Don't know _____

2. Is bilingual education different from the education provided in other classes?

   Yes _____ No _____ Don't know _____

3. If children do not speak English very well, should they be taught to read in Spanish before they are taught to read in English?

   Yes _____ No _____ Don't know _____

4. Does your child speak and understand Spanish better than he/she speaks and understands English?

   Yes _____ No _____ Don't know _____

5. Do you think that your child should be taught his/her reading lessons in Spanish or English?

   Spanish _____ English _____ Don't know _____

6. Do you feel that your child should be taught mathematics in Spanish or English?

   Spanish _____ English _____ Don't know _____

7. Do you feel that your child should be taught science in Spanish or English?

   Spanish _____ English _____ Don't know _____

8. Do you feel that the teachers spend enough time teaching the basic subjects: reading, writing, and arithmetic?

Yes _____ No _____ Don't know _____

9. Has your child ever talked with you about the fact that he/she is learning from a teacher or aide who instructs in Spanish?

Yes _____ No _____ Don't know _____

10. Do you think your child would be happier in a classroom that used only English for instructional purposes?

Yes _____ No _____ Don't know _____

11. Does your child enjoy the bilingual classroom more than he/she would enjoy a classroom conducted entirely in English?

Yes _____ No _____ Don't know _____

12. Do you think your child should remain in a bilingual-education program for more than one year?

Yes _____ No _____ Don't know _____

13. Do you think parents should visit and observe the bilingual classrooms?

Yes _____ No _____ Don't know _____

14. Does the bilingual-education program have a parent's organization?

Yes _____ No _____ Don't know _____

15. Have you attended any parent meetings conducted by the bilingual-education program or a parent advisory council?

Yes _____ No _____ Don't know _____

16. Have you received any written information in Spanish about your child's progress in school?

Yes _____ No _____ Don't know _____

17. Would you like to receive information about your child that is written in Spanish or English?

Spanish _____ English _____ Don't know _____

18. Do you think your school should teach children about Hispanic history and culture, as well as American history?

Yes _____   No _____   Don't know _____

Appendix H

Encuesta de la actitud de los padres
Versión en Español

Por favor, contesten las siguientes preguntas marcando su respuesta (✓) en la columna apropiada (sí–no). Si no saben la respuesta marquen la columna (no sé).

	Sí	No	No Sé
1. ¿Está su niño participando en una clase bilingüe?			
2. ¿Piensa Ud. que la educación bilingüe es diferente a la educación que se ofrece en una clase regular?			
3. Si su niño no habla inglés bien ¿cree Ud. que se le debe enseñar a leer primero en español?			
4. ¿Cree Ud. que su niño habla y comprende español mejor que el inglés?			
5. ¿Cree Ud. que a su niño se le debe enseñar las matemáticas en inglés o en español?			
6. ¿Cree Ud. que a su niño se le debe enseñar a leer en inglés o en español?			
7. ¿Cree Ud. que los maestros dedican suficiente tiempo a la enseñanza de la lectura, la ortografía y las matemáticas?			
8. ¿Le ha hablado su niño acerca del hecho que él esta aprendiendo en español y en inglés con una maestra bilingüe?			

	Sí	No	No Sé
9. ¿Cree Ud. que su niño estuviera más contento participando en una clase monolingüe donde se enseña en inglés solamente?			
10. ¿Cree Ud. que su niño estuviera más contento en una clase bilingüe que en una clase monolingüe en ingles?			
11. ¿Cree Ud. que los padres deben visitar y observar las clases bilingües?			
12. ¿Cree Ud. que su niño debe quedarse en el programa de educación bilingüe más de un año?			
13. ¿Tiene el programa de educación bilingüe una organización de padres en su escuela?			
14. ¿Ha asistido Ud. a algunas de las reuniones de padres del programa bilingüe o del consejo consultivo de padres?			
15. ¿Ha recibido Ud. información escrita en español acerca del progreso de su niño en la escuela?			
16. ¿Prefiere Ud. recibir información acerca de su niño escrita en español o en inglés?			
17. ¿Les gustaría que sus niños aprendieran la historia y la cultura hispana así como la historia americana?			
18. Si un niño no habla inglés, ¿cree Ud. que debería recibir sus lecciones de ciencia en español o en inglés?			

Appendix I

Monthly Evaluation Memo

Evaluation Tasks Implemented	Evaluation Problems Encountered	Observation/Findings	Related Plans for Future Evaluations

Appendix J

Evaluation Review Instrument

Part I: Critique of the Evaluation Design

A. Objectives were written in measurable terms and included the five facets of a performance objective: target population, desired behavior, performance level, operational condition, instrument.

All _____ Many _____ Few _____ None _____

B. Product objectives were written for the project. *Products* of a program are the affective and cognitive gains demonstrated by participating students.

	Yes	No
Affective	_____	_____
Cognitive	_____	_____

C. Process objectives were written for each component of the project. *Processes* are the techniques, methods, and materials used by the program.

	Yes	No
Staff development	_____	_____
Curriculum development	_____	_____
Community and parent involvement	_____	_____
Program management	_____	_____
Instruction	_____	_____

D. Comparability

1. Comparison and program groups were comparable in terms of relevant variables.

   Always _____ Often _____ Seldom _____ Never _____

2. Pretest and posttest scores were comparable in terms of relevant variables.

   Always _____ Often _____ Seldom _____ Never _____

E. Instruments

1. Instruments chosen were relevant to the objectives selected for evaluation.

   All _____   Many _____   Few _____   None _____

2. Instruments were valid.

   All _____   Many _____   Few _____   None _____

3. Instruments were reliable.

   All _____   Many _____   Few _____   None _____

F. Locally developed instruments

1. Procedures included the development of criterion-referenced measures to assess attainment of objectives.

   Always _____   Often _____   Seldom _____   Never _____

2. Logistical arrangements (personnel, schedule, budget, etc.) were well planned.

   Always _____   Often _____   Seldom _____   Never _____

3. Plans for validating the instruments were made.

   Always _____   Often _____   Seldom _____   Never _____

4. Plans for determining the reliability of the instruments were made.

   Always _____   Often _____   Seldom _____   Never _____

G. Data collection

1. Data-collection techniques for measuring the achievement of objectives were appropriate.

   Always _____   Often _____   Seldom _____   Never _____

2. Data collection was scheduled appropriately.

   Always _____   Often _____   Seldom _____   Never _____

3. Groups were differentiated by ethnicity, language, or other appropriate criteria for data-collection purposes.

   Always _____   Often _____   Seldom _____   Never _____

4. Specifications for the selection and training of testers, observers, and interviewers for each evaluation instrument were well defined.

Always _____ Often _____ Seldom _____ Never _____

H. Data analysis

1. Proposed data tabulation and summary arrangements were appropriate.

Always _____ Often _____ Seldom _____ Never _____

2. Proposed descriptive statistics were appropriate.

Always _____ Often _____ Seldom _____ Never _____

3. There were appropriate tests of significance for data analysis.

Always _____ Often _____ Seldom _____ Never _____

I. Presentation of data

1. Deadlines for the submission of evaluation reports were appropriate in relation to evaluation activities.

Always _____ Often _____ Seldom _____ Never _____

2. The reporting schedule was closely linked to key decision-making points within the project and within the LEA.

Always _____ Often _____ Seldom _____ Never _____

3. Persons responsible for report preparation and submission were identified.

Always _____ Often _____ Seldom _____ Never _____

4. Provisions for transmitting reports to program stakeholders were made.

	Yes	No
Project management	_____	_____
Project staff	_____	_____
LEA officials	_____	_____
Parents	_____	_____
Community Groups	_____	_____

Part II: Assessment of Evaluation Activities

A. The evaluation design for the measurement of product
   objectives was implemented as planned.

	Yes	No
Affective	___	___
Cognitive	___	___

B. The evaluation design for the measurement of process
   objectives was implemented as planned.

	Yes	No
Staff development	___	___
Curriculum development	___	___
Community and parent involvement	___	___
Program management	___	___
Instruction	___	___

C. Locally developed instruments

   1. Proposed instruments were developed.

      All ___   Many ___   Few ___   None ___

   2. Proposed instruments were developed on time.

      All ___   Many ___   Few ___   None ___

   3. Instruments were developed in accordance with
      established criteria.

      All ___   Many ___   Few ___   None ___

   4. Instruments were checked for reliability.

      All ___   Many ___   Few ___   None ___

   5. Instruments were validated.

      All ___   Many ___   Few ___   None ___

D. Data collection

   1. Data collection was completed on schedule.

      Always ___   Often ___   Seldom ___   Never ___

2. Evaluators considered the unique characteristics of each instrument in data collection.

   Always _____ Often _____ Seldom _____ Never _____

3. Data-collection personnel were well trained.

   Always _____ Often _____ Seldom _____ Never _____

E. Data analysis

   1. Data tabulation and summary arrangements were appropriate.

      Always _____ Often _____ Seldom _____ Never _____

   2. Descriptive statistics were appropriate.

      Always _____ Often _____ Seldom _____ Never _____

   3. Tests of significance for data analysis were appropriate.

      Always _____ Often _____ Seldom _____ Never _____

   4. Evaluators were sensitive to factors not provided for in the evaluation design but which affected the experimental or control groups.

      Always _____ Often _____ Seldom _____ Never _____

F. Presentation of data

   1. Evaluation reports were submitted on time.

      Always _____ Often _____ Seldom _____ Never _____

   2. The format of the evaluation reports was appropriate.

      Always _____ Often _____ Seldom _____ Never _____

   3. Persons designated in the evaluation plan prepared and submitted evaluation reports.

      Always _____ Often _____ Seldom _____ Never _____

   4. Evaluation reports were submitted to program stakeholders.

	Yes	No
Project management	_____	_____
Project staff	_____	_____
LEA officials	_____	_____

Parents ____ ____

Community groups ____ ____

Part III: Evaluation Recommendations

A. The evaluators made recommendations for program modifications based on evaluation findings.

Always ____   Often ____   Seldom ____   Never ____

B. Rationale for the recommendations was provided.

.   Always ____   Often ____   Seldom ____   Never ____

C. Alternative actions or possible sources of assistance were proposed.

Always ____   Often ____   Seldom ____   Never ____

D. Specific corrective actions were recommended.

Always ____   Often ____   Seldom ____   Never ____

Appendix K

Opinionnaire: Nonprogram Teachers

The following opinionnaire, if used in an anonymous fashion, identifies negative attitudes of nonprogram teachers. If bilingual education is to succeed in a local school system, teacher support is essential. Project directors should never assume that a new bilingual program will be welcomed automatically. Rather, they need to reach out to nonprogram teachers for philosophical support.

Nonprogram teachers should receive the opinionnaire approximately six weeks after school has started. By this time, they have formulated some opinions and can respond to the bilingual program's scheduling and implementation. They should be instructed not to put their name on the form.

Opinions of Non-Bilingual Program Teachers

1. Does the scheduling of the bilingual-education program interfere with your regular plans and lessons?

   Yes _____   No _____   Don't know _____

   If "Yes," please give details:

2. Do you feel that students who participate in bilingual-education activities are missing an important part of their education?

   Yes _____   No _____   Don't know _____

   If "Yes," why?

3. Do you feel that the students from the local Hispanic com-

munity are so far behind when they enter school that bilingual education will not do much to help them?

Yes _____   No _____   Don't know _____

4. Have your Hispanic students who participate in bilingual-education activities demonstrated:

    Improved academic growth rates?
    Yes _____   No _____   Don't know _____
    Improved discipline?
    Yes _____   No _____   Don't know _____
    Improved self-image?
    Yes _____   No _____   Don't know _____

5. Should non-English-speaking first graders be involved in Spanish or English reading-readiness activities?

    English _____   Spanish _____   Don't know _____

Appendix L

Principal's Survey

The following questionnaire can be used to collect data from principals who have bilingual programs in their buildings. Like the questionnaire for nonprogram teachers, it can be used to identify negative attitudes. These kinds of difficulties interfere with program management and can be especially damaging to the implementation of new programs.

I. In-service

    A. Were you invited to the in-service sessions held by the bilingual-education program?

    Yes _____   No _____

    B. Did you make any recommendations regarding the scope or direction of the in-service component of the bilingual-education program?

    Yes _____   No _____

    C. Do you feel you should have been involved in the planning of the in-service component?

    Yes _____   No _____

    D. What activities do you feel should have been included in the in-service component that were omitted?

II. Curriculum Development

    A. Did you participate in curriculum planning for the bilingual-education program?

    Yes _____   No _____

    B. Were you informed of the specific content areas that

would be emphasized in curricula for the bilingual-education program?

Yes _____ No _____

C. How do you perceive the role of the principal in curriculum development and planning?

D. How do you perceive the role of the principal in curriculum development and planning as it relates to bilingual education?

III. Program Activities and Staffing

A. How have you been involved with bilingual-education teachers?

B. Did you receive prior notice regarding tests to be given to bilingual children in your school?

Yes _____ No _____

C. Have you met with bilingual-program teachers in your building?

Yes _____ No _____

D. Have you met with bilingual-program aides in your building?

Yes _____ No _____

E. Have bilingual-program teachers or aides contacted you directly regarding any problems they have had?

Yes _____   No _____

F. Have bilingual-program teachers or aides solicited your advice on any issues relating to bilingual education or your school?

Yes _____   No _____

G. Do you feel you could be more involved with bilingual-program teachers and aides in your school by meeting with them individually or in groups?

Yes _____   No _____

IV. Parent Advisory Council

A. Have you been invited to any PAC meetings in your school?

Yes _____   No _____

B. Have you attended any PAC meetings in your school?

Yes _____   No _____

C. How many bilingual-program parents have you talked with (either directly or by phone) since September? _____

D. What are your attitudes about parental involvement in your school?

in bilingual education?

E. Have you requested meetings with parents of bilingual-program children?

Yes _____   No _____

V. Management

A. Are you aware of federal and state legislation regarding bilingual education?

Yes _____ No _____

B. Have you met with bilingual program administrators?

Yes _____ No _____

If yes, how many times since September, and with whom?

C. What areas, if any, of the bilingual program do you feel need strengthening?

D. What particular area of the bilingual program do you feel you have the most contact with?

E. Are you provided with any of the reports published by the bilingual program?

Yes _____ No _____

If yes, which ones?

F. How would you rate your involvement with bilingual-program administrators?

Very high _____ About average _____ Very low _____

Appendix M

Evaluation Contract

This evaluation contract can be used or adapted as a legal agreement between a local school system's bilingual-education program and the contracted evaluator, whether a corporation, a university, or an individual. Of course, the local program should seek legal counsel before using the contract.

THIS AGREEMENT, entered into as of this _____ day of _____(month) _____(year), by and between the School District of _____ and _____ of _____

WITNESSETH THAT

WHEREAS, the _____ School District received a grant under Title VII of public law 89-10 (as amended) of the Elementary and Secondary Education Act (hereinafter referred to as the ESEA, said Grant designated as the Bilingual Education Program.) Grant Number: _____.

WHEREAS, pursuant to said Grant the _____ _____ School District is undertaking certain activities as identified in the submitted project.

WHEREAS, the _____ School District desires to engage _____ (hereinafter referred to as the Evaluator) to render certain assistance as identified in the Statement of Work.

NOW, THEREFORE, the _____ School District and _____ mutually agree as follows:

1. The Evaluator shall in a satisfactory and proper manner as agreed to by the _____ School District perform an evaluation of the Title VII program as per requirements set by the United States Office of Education and the evaluation design which was submitted in _____ (month) of _____(year).

2. The Evaluator shall commence performance on
_____(month, day), _____(year) and shall
complete performance no later than _____.

3. The Evaluator shall prepare an evaluation relating to
the accomplishment of the project objectives by means of statistical analyses, observations, interviews, and such other
evaluating and reporting techniques as shall be agreed to by
the Project.

4. The Evaluator shall review the approved Project and
other pertinent information to determine evaluating and
reporting procedures pertinent to the Bilingual-Education
Program as established by the Program, the State Department
of Education, and the United States Office of Education. The
Evaluator shall prepare and perform a comprehensive evaluation to meet the evaluating and reporting requirements of the
United States Office of Education and _____
School District.

5. All data, information, preliminary reports, and final
reports from the Evaluator shall remain the property of the
_____ School District.

6. Decisions for all publications and release for information connected with this Agreement will conform with OE dissemination guidelines and _____ School Dis-
trict during and after the time of this agreement.

7. The _____ School District agrees to
make available to the Evaluator:

    a. The results of all standardized tests given on a
       district-wide basis for all schools in the Bilingual-
       Education Program and all control schools.

    b. The results of all testing of _____
       District children under Title I or other specialized
       programs.

    c. The assistance of project personnel and other person-
       nel in the administration of instruments.

    d. Access to past attendance records of the
       _____ School District.

8. The following dates represent deadlines for various
aspects of the evaluation by _____, the
Evaluator:

Item 1	_____	Completion of revised prelim-inary evaluation design and objectives
Item 2	_____	Collection of baseline data
Item 3	_____	Interim Evaluation Report
Item 4	_____	Post-testing data results
Item 5	_____	Final Evaluation Report

9. It is expressly understood and agreed that the amount due and payable by the Program is not to exceed $_____ and is to include all costs and expenses related to this Agreement and represents payment in full for the complete and satisfactory services noted herein.

Using funds received under Grant #_____, the Program shall make payment under this Agreement in accordance with the following method, such payment to be made upon presentation of a requisition for payment by _____, the Evaluator.

Payments shall be made according to the following schedule:

    a. Upon satisfactory completion of Item 1 of Section 8 above the Evaluator shall present a requisition to the Program in the amount of $_____.

    b. Upon satisfactory completion of Item 2 of Section 8 above, the Evaluator shall present a requisition to the Program in the amount of $_____.

    c. Upon satisfactory completion of Item 3 of Section 8 above, the Evaluator shall present a requisition to the Program in the amount of $_____.

    d. Upon satisfactory completion of Items 4 and 5 of Section 8 above, the Evaluator shall present a requisition to the Program in the amount of $_____.

For each week that Item 4 of Section 8 is overdue in submission, $100.00 shall be deducted from the total payment amount.

Ten copies of completed data analysis and evaluation reports shall be submitted in the quantity required by the Project.

10. _____ School District shall maintain such records and accounts, including property, personal, and financial records related to this Agreement, as are deemed necessary to the Office of Education to assure a proper accounting for all project funds. These records shall be made available at any time for audit purposes to the Program, the State Department of Education, the United States Office of Education or any authorized representative of them and will be retained for five years after the expiration of the Agreement, unless permission to destroy them is granted by the State Department of Education and the United States Office of Education.

11. The Evaluator agrees that all personal data obtained by its employees in this Agreement shall be kept absolutely confidential.

12. _____ School District agrees not to use the name of the Evaluator or any members of the Evaluator's staff in promotion or advertising, or in any other form of publicity without the written permission of the Evaluator.

13. The Evaluator agrees to consider such additional conditions requested by the Project consistent with the Grant and any additional conditions governing the use of ESEA Title VII funds or performance of Title VII programs as may be required by law, by executive order, by regulation or by other policy announced by the United States Office of Education.

14. The Evaluator agrees to assist the _____ School District in complying with all the conditions governing Grants under the Elementary and Secondary Education Act of 1965, and all other laws, regulations and orders which may govern the use of ESEA Title VII funds as the same may be amended or changed from time to time.

15. The work statement for this evaluation shall consist of the evaluation design submitted with the Federal application and revised under Item 1 of the deliverable end items (see paragraph 8). The design, upon agreement in writing between the Project Director and _____, the Evaluator, shall be flexible and may change from time to time depending upon the program's needs.

16. Should the evaluator default on any one of the conditions agreed herein, the _____ School District

shall have the option to cancel the contract upon a 60 day written notice.

17. Budget design

_____ days of _____ @ ____ / day	_____
_____ days of _____ @ ____ / day	_____
_____ days of _____ @ ____ / day	_____
_____ days of _____ @ ____ / day	_____

Data analysis costs _____

Tests, surveys, and reports _____

TOTAL _____

18. Grantee is not relinquishing administrative control of the project.

19. All provisions of rules and regulations governing Office of Education Title VII Bilingual Programs not written into this agreement shall prevail including 45 CFR 100 and the special grant terms and conditions attached to Grant #_____.

20. Development and production of audiovisual materials, questionnaires, surveys, etc. are not authorized until prior written approval is received from the grant officer.

IN WITNESS WHEREOF, the parties hereto have set their hands by proper persons duly authorized on this date,

_____ for _____ School District
(Name of Contractor)

for _____
(Name of Evaluator)

By _____   By _____
(signature)   *(signature)*

_____   _____
(type name)   *(type name)*

                            _____
                               (type title)

Appendix N

Class List

Evaluators and educators maintaining records related to bilingual instruction should keep two separate lists, one identifying youngsters who receive primary instruction in English and another identifying youngsters who receive primary instruction in Spanish. The program may choose to have more than two categories (English dominant, Spanish dominant, English transitional, bilingual, etc.).

	English Dominant		Spanish Dominant
1		1	
2		2	
3		3	
4		4	
5		5	
6		6	
7		7	
8		8	
9		9	
10		10	
11		11	
12		12	
13		13	
14		14	
15		15	
16		16	
17		17	
18		18	
19		19	
20		20	

English Dominant		Spanish Dominant	
21		21	
22		22	
23		23	
24		24	
25		25	
26		26	

Appendix O

Classroom Visitation Form

Program evaluators should maintain records of classroom
visits. Completed copies of this form can be given to management or kept as evaluation records. In each box on the right
the evaluator writes the date of the visit above the slash and
his or her initials below the slash.

School	Tutor-Teacher	Dates visited/Evaluator				

Appendix P

Evaluation Workshops

The following outline describes several topics the evaluation team may wish to present at workshops. The purpose of the meetings is to:

- ☐ Inform teachers about evaluation activities
- ☐ Encourage teacher participation in evaluation activities
- ☐ Give teachers an opportunity to develop their own instruments
- ☐ Make teachers more receptive to evaluation recommendations

The topics are general, since the workshops will be the first time some teachers, especially paraprofessionals, are introduced to measurement, statistics, and testing. Each session should be limited to one or two hours. All the topics listed can be covered in 12 to 15 hours of meetings.

Testing in a Bilingual Environment

- ☐ Definition of bilingual education
- ☐ Definition of language dominance
- ☐ Rationale for bilingual education and the relationship of this rationale to program evaluation and individualized testing
- ☐ Values-clarification exercises that involve discussions of language dominance, testing, bilingual education, etc.
- ☐ Relationship between bilingual-education testing and individualized-instruction testing (diagnostic/ prescriptive)
- ☐ Difference between program evaluation and testing for instruction
- ☐ Philosophical differences that affect actual test development

Performance Objectives, Testing, and Evaluation

- ☐ A taxonomic approach to the development of performance objectives

- ☐ Using operational conditions as part of objectives
- ☐ Including measurement in an objective
- ☐ Defining highly specific target populations within objectives (individualizing goals)
- ☐ Presenting objectives and their related evaluation procedures
- ☐ Writing product and process objectives
- ☐ Relating performance objectives to actual classroom processes

Teachers should first write hypothetical objectives in groups and then write product and process goals for their own activities.

Research Designs

- ☐ Presentation and discussion of different design patterns (pre-post, two groups; pre-post, one group; post-post, two groups with random selection; etc.)
- ☐ Brief introduction to measurement devices within these various research patterns (grade equivalencies, t-tests, etc.)

Review of Available Instruments

During this session, the workshop participant reviews a series of instruments and discusses strengths and weaknesses ranging from graphic presentation to reliability. The following questions should be discussed: What are we measuring? Who can administer the test? Who was it normed on? etc.

- ☐ *Inter-American Series*
- ☐ Puerto Rican Department of Instruction series
- ☐ Standardized tests (*Metropolitan, Stanford*, etc.)
- ☐ Self-concept scales
- ☐ Early childhood tests (*Walker Readiness, Metro Readiness*, etc.)
- ☐ Secondary instruments
- ☐ Parent questionnaires
- ☐ Management-evaluation techniques

Appendix Q

Evaluation-Team Protocol

Frequently, program evaluators are graduate students or professors who have never been classroom teachers or program administrators. These suggestions may seem elementary and even insulting to some, but the reader should bear in mind that there are program evaluators throughout the country who need a refresher on school-building protocol.

1. Since evaluation schedules are planned a few months in advance, it is a good idea to call the project director four or five days before each scheduled visit to confirm your appointment and to reschedule if necessary.
2. Before going to the classrooms, check in with the project director or secretary so they know you have arrived. They can notify you if there are last-minute changes.
3. When you arrive in a classroom, always ask the teacher if it is all right to sit in on the lesson. Generally, he or she will not object, but if the teacher prefers that you leave, ask for a more convenient appointment.
4. Avoid taking notes during a lesson. Write down your observations after you leave the room.
5. Before leaving, try to give the teacher a few words of feedback. If you have a suggestion, phrase it in a positive fashion, not a supervisory one.
6. Try not to leave the classroom until the presented lesson has been completed.
7. Talk with the project director before you leave the building. Give highlights of what you have observed, both negative and positive. If the project director would like a written report, advise him or her that all written feedback is given in the monthly memo prepared by the evaluation team.
8. If an emergency arises and you cannot keep an appointment, call ahead so that a substitute can make the visit or so it can be rescheduled.
9. Don't visit a program without knowing its philosophy, goals, and procedures.

Instruments and Instructional Materials

Name and Author	Source
APELL Test: Assessment Program of Early Learning Levels, by Eleanor V. Cochran and James L. Shannon	Edcodyne 1 City Blvd. West, Suite 935 Orange, CA 92668
BABEL Language Test, developed by BABEL Bilingual Program	BABEL Bilingual Program Berkeley Unified School District 1414 Walnut Street Berkeley, CA 94709
BARSIT: Barranquilla Rapid Survey Intelligence Test, by Francisco del Olmo	Psychological Corp. 304 E. 45th Street New York, NY 10017
Bilingual Education Applied Research Unit (BEARU) System for Learning and Assessment of Science in Spanish: Elementary Level Science Objectives for Bilingual Classes, by Marietta Saravia Shore, Liza Martínez de Gómez, Dr. Mary Graeber, Alan Ehrlich, and Roselin Ehrlich	Bilingual Education Applied Research Unit (BEARU) Hunter College 466 Lexington New York, NY 10017
BINL: Basic Inventory of Natural Language, by Charles H. Herbert	CHECpoint Systems, Inc. 1558 N. Waterman Ave., Suite C San Bernardino, CA 92404
Boehm Test of Basic Concepts, by Anne E. Boehm	Psychological Corp. 304 E. 45th Street New York, NY 10017
BSM: Bilingual Syntax Measure, by Marina K. Burt, Heidi C. DuLay, and Eduardo Hernández Ch.	Psychological Corp. 757 3rd Avenue New York, NY 10017
California Preschool Social Competency Scale, by Samuel Levine, Freeman F. Elzey, and Mary Lewis	Consulting Psychologist Press, Inc. 577 College Avenue Palo Alto, CA 94306

Name and Author	Source

Canales Spanish Reading Readiness Test, by Carman Canales

BABEL Bilingual Program
Berkeley Unified School
  District
1414 Walnut Street
Berkeley, CA 94709

Comprehensive Tests of Basic Skills (CTBS)

CTB/McGraw-Hill
Del Monte Research Park
Monterey, CA 93940

Cultural Attitude Inventories, by Perry A. Zirkel and Stephan L. Jackson

Teaching Resources
50 Pond Park Road
Hingham, MA 02043

Cultural Attitude Scales, by Perry A. Zirkel and Stephan L. Jackson

Teaching Resources
50 Pond Park Road
Hingham, MA 02043

Del Rio Language Screening Test

National Educational
  Laboratory Publishers, Inc.
P.O. Box 1003
Austin, TX 78767

Denver Developmental Screening Test, by William K. Frankenburg, Josiah B. Dodds, and Alma W. Fandal

Ladoca Project and
  Publishing Foundation, Inc.
E. 51st Ave. and Lincoln St.
Denver, CO 80216

Diagnostic Reading Scales, by George Spache

CTB/McGraw-Hill
Del Monte Research Park
Monterey, CA 93940

Dos Amigos Verbal Language Scale, by Donald E. Critchlow, Ph.D.

Academic Therapy
  Publications
1539 4th Street
P.O. Box 899
San Rafael, CA 94901

Gates-McKillop Reading Diagnostic Tests, by Arthur I. Gates and Anne S. McKillop

Teachers College Press
1234 Amsterdam Avenue
New York, NY 10027

Geist Picture Interest Inventory, by Harold Geist

Western Psychological
  Services
12031 Wilshire Blvd.
Los Angeles, CA 90025

*The Gloria & David Oral Language
Assessment*, by M. Reyes Mazon,
Ph.D.

Language Arts
  Associates, Inc.
Suite 6 4670 Nebo Drive
La Mesa, CA 92041

IMAR Bilingual Attitude Scale, by
Ivan Marleaux

Ivan Marleaux
19009 E. Lake Drive
Country Club of
Miami, FLA 33015

Inter-American Series: Tests of General Ability, by Herschel T. Manuel

Guidance Testing Associates
St. Mary's University
1 Camino Santa Maria
San Antonio, TX 78284

Inter-American Series: Comprehension of Oral Language, by Herschel
T. Manuel

Guidance Testing Associates
St. Mary's University
1 Camino Santa Maria
San Antonio, TX 78284

*Inter-American Series: Tests of
Reading*, by Herschel T. Manuel

Guidance Testing Associates
St. Mary's University
1 Camino Santa Maria
San Antonio, TX 78284

IPAT Culture Fair Intelligence Test,
by Raymond B. Cattell and A.K.S.
Cattell

Institute for Personality and
  Ability Testing
1602 Coronado Drive
Champaign, IL 61820

James Language Dominance Test, by
Peter James

Teaching Resources
50 Pond Park Road
Hingham, MA 02043

*John T. Dailey Language Facility
Test*, by John T. Dailey

Allington Corp.
801 N. Pitt Street #701
Alexandria, VA 22314

Kraner Preschool Math Inventory,
by Robert E. Kraner

Teaching Resources
50 Pond Park Road
Hingham, MA 02043

*Los Angeles Developmental Reading
Program*, developed by Bilingual
Education Program, Los Angeles
Unified School District

Paul S. Amidon
  & Associates, Inc.
1966 Benson Avenue
St. Paul, Minnesota 55116

Name and Author	Source
McDaniel's Inferred Self-Concept Scale, by Dr. Elizabeth McDaniel	Western Psychological Services 12031 Wilshire Blvd. Los Angeles, CA 90023
Metropolitan Readiness Tests, by Gertrude H. Hildreth, Nellie L. Griffiths, and Mary E. McGauvran	Harcourt, Brace, Jovanovich, Inc. 757 Third Avenue New York, NY 10017
Oral English Proficiency Placement Test, by Steve Moreno, Ph.D.	Moreno Educational Company 7050 Belle Glade Lane San Diego, CA 92119
Oral Language Dominance Measure, developed by El Paso Public School District	Department of Curriculum and Staff Development El Paso Public Schools 6531 Boeing Drive El Paso, TX 79925
Oral Language Evaluation, by Dr. Nicholas J. Silvaroli, J.O. Maynes, Ph.D., and Jann Skinner, Ph.D.	EMC Corp. 180 E. 6th Street St. Paul, Minnesota 55101
Oral Spanish Proficiency Placement Test, by Steve Moreno, Ph.D.	Moreno Educational Company 7050 Belle Glade Lane San Diego, CA 92119
Peabody Picture Vocabulary Test, by Lloyd M. Dunn	American Guidance Service, Inc. Publishers Building Circle Pines, MN 55014
Pictorial Test of Bilingualism and Language Dominance, by Darwin Nelson, Michael Fellner, and C. L. Norrell	Texas Testing Services, Inc. 401 Poenisch Corpus Christi, TX
Piers-Harris Children's Self-Concept Scale, by Ellen V. Piers and Dale B. Harris	Counselor Recordings and Tests Box 6184, Acklen Station Nashville, TN 37212

Por el mundo del cuento y la
aventura

Laidlaw Brothers, Publishers
Thatcher and Madison
River Forest, IL 60305

Primary Self-Concept Inventory,
by Douglas Muller and Robert
Leonetti

Teaching Resources
50 Pond Park Road
Hingham, MA 02043

Prueba de lectura

Oficina de Evaluación
Departamento de Instrucción
  Pública
Hato Rey, Puerto Rico

Pruebas de lectura en español

Oficina de Evaluación
Departamento de Instrucción
  Pública
Hato Rey, Puerto Rico

ROLL (Region One Literacy Lessons)

Melton Book Company
111 Leslie Street
Dallas, TX 75207

San Bernardino Language Domi-
nance Survey, developed by the San
Bernardino Unified School District

Bilingual Office
San Bernardino Unified
  School District
799 North F Street
San Bernardino, CA 92510

Santillana Bilingual Series Mastery
Tests

Santillana Publishing
  Company
575 Lexington Avenue
New York, NY 10022

Santillana Bilingual Series Program
Management System

Santillana Publishing
  Company
575 Lexington Avenue
New York, NY 10022

School Attitude Tests, by Earl
McCallon and Juan Rivera

Teaching Resources
50 Pond Park Road
Hingham, MA 02043

Screening Test of Spanish Grammar,
by Allen Toronto

Northwestern University
  Press
1735 Benson St.
Evanston, IL 60201

Self-Esteem Inventory, by Dr.
Stanley Coopersmith

Self-Esteem Institute
934 Dewing
LaFayette, CA 94549

SOBER (System for Objectives-Based Evaluation of Reading)

Science Research Associates
259 E. Erie Street
Chicago, IL 60611

Spanish-English Dominance Assessment Scale, by Bernard Spolsky and Penny Murphy (Set A of Tests in Microfiche)

Educational Testing Service
Test Collection
Princeton, NJ 08540

SRA Reading Program

Science Research Associates
259 E. Erie Street
Chicago, IL 60611

Stanford Early School Achievement Test, by Eric F. Gardner, Jack C. Merwin, Robert Callis, and Richard Madden

Harcourt, Brace,
  Jovanovich, Inc.
757 Third Avenue
New York, NY 10017

STAR: Screening Test of Academic Readiness, by A. Edward Ahr

Priority Innovations, Inc.
P.O. Box 792
Skokie, IL 60076

Survey of Study Habits and Attitudes, by W.F. Brown and W.H. Holtzman

Psychological Corp.
304 E. 45th Street
New York, NY 10017

Test de destrezas básicas en lecturas

Oficina de Evaluación
Departamento de Instrucción
  Pública
Hato Rey, Puerto Rico

Test for Auditory Comprehension of Language, by Elizabeth Carrow-Woolfolk

Teaching Resources
50 Pond Park Road
Hingham, MA 02043

Test of Oral Language Proficiency, by Louise Michael and Dr. John Salazar

Southwestern Cooperative
  Education Laboratory
229 Truman N.E.
Albuquerque, NM 87108

Name and Author	Source
Test of Basic Experiences (TOBE), by Margaret H. Moss	CTB/McGraw-Hill Del Monte Research Park Monterey, CA 93940
Vocabulary Comprehension Scale, by Tina E. Bangs	Teaching Resources 50 Pond Park Road Hingham, MA 02043
Walker Readiness Test for Disadvantaged Preschool Children, by Wanda Walker ERIC No: ED-045-736	Bureau of Research U.S. Office of Education Washington, D.C.
Woodcock-Johnson Psycho-Educational Battery, by Richard W. Woodcock and Mary Bonner Johnson	Teaching Resources 50 Pond Park Road Hingham, MA 02043

Bibliography

Andersson, Theodore, and Mildred Boyer. *Bilingual Schooling in the United States*. Detroit: Blaine Ethridge Books, 1976.

Buell, Kenneth. *An Annotated List of Tests for Spanish Speakers*. Princeton, N.J.: Educational Testing Service, Inc., 1973.

Buros, Oscar Kristen. *Tests in Print II: An Index to Tests, Test Reviews, and the Literature on Specific Tests*. Highland Park, N.J.: The Gryphon Press, 1974.

Evaluation Echoes: A Teacher's Guide for Selecting Bilingual Education Materials. Trenton, N.J.: Puerto Rican Congress of New Jersey, 1976.

Evaluation Instruments for Bilingual Education: An Annotated Bibliography. Austin, Tex.: Dissemination and Assessment Center for Bilingual Education, 1974.

Huxley, Renira, and Elizabeth Ingram, eds. *Language Acquisition: Models and Methods*. New York: Academic Press, 1971.

Selector's Guide for Bilingual Education Materials, vols. I and II. EPIE Reports nos. 73 and 74. New York: EPIE Institute, 1976.

Silverman, Robert J., Joslyn K. Noa, and Randall H. Russell. *Oral Language Tests for Bilingual Students: An Evaluation of Language Dominance and Proficiency Instruments*. Portland, Ore.: Northwest Regional Educational Laboratory, 1976.

Simon, Sidney et al. *Values Clarification: A Handbook of Practical Strategies for Teachers and Students*. New York: Hart, 1972.